Here Come the Marines

Memoirs
of
Billy Godfrey
WWII Carrier Marine

Order this book online at www.trafford.com
or email orders@trafford.com

Most Trafford titles are also available at major online book retailers.

Note for Librarians: A cataloguing record for this book is available from Library and Archives Canada at www.collectionscanada.ca/amicus/index-e.html

Printed in Victoria, BC, Canada.

ISBN: 978-1-4269-1315-0

Our mission is to efficiently provide the world's finest, most comprehensive book publishing service, enabling every author to experience success. To find out how to publish your book, your way, and have it available worldwide, visit us online at www.trafford.com

Trafford rev. 08/18/09

www.trafford.com

North America & international
toll-free: 1 888 232 4444 (USA & Canada)
phone: 250 383 6864 • fax: 812 355 4082

Billy Godfrey
New Bern, N.C.
June, 1944

Interviews of Billy Godfrey

Transcribed by Joe Frank Rinehart

Production Manager: Bruce Behner

Manuscript Preparation: E. Amelia Billingsley

Manuscript Editing: Brent Behner

Photograph Preservation: Hilary Tang

FOREWORD

This is a book of Billy Godfrey's personal memoirs, originally recorded by Joe Frank Rinehart in 2007 and 2008. I met Billy as a member of the Marine Corps League, the oldest Marine of our Detachment in Rome, Georgia. At my first meeting, he got up and sang one of his infamous ballads which brought out hearty laughter. Billy is a man who delights in humor and story telling. How many people in Marine Corps boot camp get into trouble for laughing?

Many of you reading this book know Billy. Even if you know him well, his story deserves to be told here. When asked to tell me what he did after discharge from the Marines, he said, "I was pretty wild, and soon after getting out I bought a '40 Ford and rolled it over." He married on Valentine's Day of 1947 while pursuing his education through the GI Bill. The State of Alabama wanted educators to work with veterans returning from the war. With a high school diploma and a minimum of three years farming experience, Billy could become a Veterans Vocational Agriculture teacher. He was the first chosen for the program and worked for 6 years, receiving $2000 dollars a year plus $350 mileage pay. Working with a caseload of 20 ex-servicemen by day and going to college by night, Billy graduated in 1957 after attending the University of Alabama, Gadsden, and Jacksonville State University.

Billy then taught history and science at the self-contained school in Alexis, Alabama. He admitted to having difficulty knowing what to do with students. But, as his story tells, he had learned all the tricks of a school boy long ago. He insists they were not mean students, just full of devilment. "I hated a quiet classroom so I would tell a joke, and it would help make them want to learn." One way to teach them was to have them learn to read music and to assemble a choir. Some of his most difficult charges were boys who could sing some pretty good bass. These boys always wanted song with bass leads. The choir became quite popular around the community with demand becoming almost too much for them to keep pace.

Billy then moved to Centre Middle School in Alabama where he taught physical education and coached football. When he moved on to Harding Junior High to teach and coach for 6 years, he took the basketball team from several years of total losses to a feared team in the area. He returned to the Alexis school as principal for the final 8 years of the school's existence. Then it was to Cedar Bluff, Alabama, where he taught 7th grade Science and 9th grade Physical Education. He also coached girls' varsity basketball and boys' junior varsity basketball and football.

After retirement from teaching, he decided to run for the local school board in 1981. "I figured I taught 1,000 students, and if I got them and their spouses to vote for me, I was in!" He easily won the election twice, serving 12 years on the board. "If I had known I would live this long, I would have run again," was his wry observation at his retirement from public service.

Billy Godfrey has a strong faith and church loyalty. He has been a song director for about 60 years and has taught Sunday School for much of that time. He describes his church as "a country church where, once you got in a job, you stayed."

Anyone who has ever met Billy can easily see the number of years of service to his faith, to young people, and to his community and realize that he is indeed a very special person. His service to others for 47 years in education and more than 60 years as a church leader demonstrate the character of the man. Take a bus trip with Billy to Parris Island, S.C., and his jokes and stories will entertain an entire bus full of former Marines as they revisit the site of youthful but not forgotten boot camp experiences. You'll find this man of 90 years standing at the front of the bus leading old Gospel songs with every man on that bus singing along. They listen closely for the verse they may not recall, knowing that Billy will remind them of every word.

Billy offers this Recipe for a Long Life:

- Laugh a lot
- Don't worry about things you cannot change
- Take exercise
- Have a good relationship with Jesus Christ

Billy Godfrey, thank you for sharing your part of history.

Semper Fidelis

Bruce L. Behner

Contents

Chapter One

GROWING UP

My name is Billy Godfrey. I was born in Alexis community, Cherokee, Alabama. I'm an old World War II Marine, Serial Number 946928.

There were eight children in our family. We were cotton farmers. We had to pick cotton, chop cotton, hoe cotton, and plow cotton with those old mules all day long.

One day I was plowing with mules in a field alongside a road and a good looking lady came by in a convertible. She stopped and asked, "Young man, do you have the time?"

I answered, "Yes, ma'am. But, I don't have nobody to hold these mules."

We boys were, I guess, a little bit mean and full of devilment. We lived next to a school. It was a three-teacher school. The principal was a man and he had a fire box filled with sand which he used to show the class how to plow terraces, etc. He would use his finger as a plow in making the furrow for the demonstration.

One weekend a boy named Clyde Rinehart (father of Joe Frank) came in and played a trick on the principal. Clyde got up on the sand table and had deposited a turd in the box. The next Monday, the teacher was working at the sand table, using his finger to demonstrate plowing. Suddenly his finger hit something foreign and he stopped, looking shocked. Clyde gave himself away when he said, "Must have hit a stump!" We all wanted to laugh but were afraid to do so.

During Valentine week the students would bring in cards and place them in a box. Then on Thursday we would have a party and the Valentines would be distributed. Over the weekend after the party, my brother June and I slipped into the school and messed in the box. Monday morning the box was stinking and the teacher told some of the boys to carry it to the woods. Estelle, one of the girls in the class, said that if they were going to throw the box away, she would like to have it. The teacher could not make her understand that she really didn't want the box and wouldn't tell Estelle why. Estelle almost cried because she could not have that box.

My brother June, B.G. Poole, Jadie Price, Arthur Waddell, Lamar Gossett, June Gossett, W. M. Anderson, and I would hang out at the country store when we didn't have anything else to do. B.G. was always the clown of the bunch. One Sunday afternoon we wanted some candy, but none of us had any money. We talked B.G. into buying the candy. Mr. Walsh Arnold ran the store. We told B.G. to buy the candy and when he had it, he was to feel all through his pockets and tell Mr. Walsh that he had lost his money. We figured that Mr. Walsh would tell him to take the candy and pay later. B.G. didn't want to do that but we talked him into it. It was a hot afternoon and Mr. and Mrs. Arnold with several other people were sitting outside the store in a shady spot. B.G. told Mr. Arnold, "I want in the store."

Mr. Arnold told his wife to wait on the young man. We knew then that our plan was doomed. We were standing around kind of snickering and B.G. stepped up to the counter and ordered his candy. He was searching through his pockets and said, "I lost my money."

Mrs. Arnold said, "Well, you won't get any candy."

When we got out of there, B.G. cussed us out.

B.G. never had to work like most of the boys growing up in Alexis at that time. In fact, his uncle, Tol Price, nicknamed him "Dodger" because B.G. was always able to dodge work. B.G.'s father, Ben Poole, died of cancer when B.G. was fifteen years old. Although he was old enough and strong enough to take on the work of the farm, B.G.'s family hired a young black man, Knee Fife, to work the crop the year that Ben died. Knee and the Price brothers, Jadie and Clarence (called Tex) often worked together in the work of planting, etc. They would plant the crop for the Price family and then would move to the Poole crop. Although B.G. was around, he seldom helped with the work.

One day they asked B.G. to help with the work and, of course, he refused. One of them said, "Well, at least go get us some cool water."

B.G. went for the water and put it into a clear glass jug. Very carefully, he placed some flour in the bottom of the jug. He handed the jug to Knee and after Knee had drunk, B.G. seemed to have a fit of conscience and said, "I'm sorry...I put arsenic in that jug."

Jadie, Tex, and Knee saw the flour in the bottom of the jug and assumed that B.G. was telling the truth. Knee gagged and coughed and tried to throw up. He just knew that he was going to die. B.G. finally told them that it was only flour in the bottom of the jug. Eventually Knee saw the humor of the joke and he and B.G. were lifelong friends. Shortly before B.G. died, Knee laughed and told the story to Joe Frank Rinehart.

Another time, we were at the Poole home. B.G. had a young bull. It was a pretty good sized bull but was just a yearling. B.G. suggested that we try riding that bull. I said that I would ride it, but first I wanted to try it out in the stall. The plan was for me to get on the bull, and my brother June was to hold the door. I should have known better! As soon as I got on the bull, he made a circle and June threw the door open. The bull headed for the door, jumped over the sill, and I fell off, landing right on my back across the raised sill. It was probably a good thing that I fell for if the bull had got into the lot, he might have killed me.

In the summer when the crops were laid by, we swam in the Coosa River just about every day. The river was about a mile from our house, and we'd walk down there and swim as a way to stay cool. We did not have swim suits but would just go "skinny dipping." One day, B.G. took off his overalls and hung them on a limb overhanging the water. A strong wind came up and blew his pants into the river. There they went, floating down the river. None of us wore underwear, just a shirt and overalls. So, B.G. had nothing but a shirt to wear home. He had to tie that little shirt around him and walk home with it tied around his waist. He looked comical and we laughed at him as we walked along. When we got to the main road, we met Mrs. Holcomb and her three daughters. B.G. walked on home, wearing that shirt.

We didn't have any money, but we had fun!

One time my parents went to town. The older children were looking after the younger children. I would not behave so they put me out of the house and locked the doors. We had an old cow bell down at the barn. I went down there and got the bell. I came back and ran around the house ringing the bell and yelling, "The house is on fire! The house is on fire!"

I looked up and neighbors were coming from both sides. A heavy set woman ran all the way to our house, and she wanted to know what was wrong? The other kids said, "It was just Billy, acting foolish."

The woman made a grab for me and I went under the house. When my parents came home, I got on fire!

In the summertime when the crops were laid by, the churches would have revivals with both day and night services. One time I told my Dad that I was going to a service. I came home with two black eyes. Dad wanted to know how I got them. I told him that when we stood to sing, a lady in the bench in front of me had her dress stuck in her butt so I reached up to pull it out. She turned around and blacked my left eye.

Dad said, "Well, that explains one eye. What happened to the other one?"

I said, "Well, I figured she must have wanted it like it was so I put it back. That's when she blacked my right eye."

I was twelve years old when the Depression came. It was a terrible time. Some folks lost everything they had. Some even committed suicide. It didn't bother us much. We didn't have anything to lose. A lot of folks went hungry. Some had three meals a day: corn meal, oat meal, and miss-a-meal. My family always had plenty to eat. But, city folks were in much worse circumstances. They were just about starving to death and had to get into soup lines. But our family butchered three hogs. We had milk cows, and we had corn to carry to the grist mill to make corn meal. So, we were okay. We had plenty of milk, cornbread, and good old turnip greens.

The economy got so bad that they had to close the schools because they didn't have any money to pay the teachers. People had bought Model T Fords and they didn't have money to buy gasoline. Some people removed the front end and installed shafts, thus making a horse-drawn cart. These were called "Hoover Carts." My friend had one of these converted carts. We would take turns using different mules to pull the cart and ride around the community. Occasionally, we would get the girls to ride with us.

People maintained their sense of humor about things. There was a joke going around about a man going to the dentist. The man was told that he had pyorrhea. The man said, "Doc, I may have pyorrhea, but I haven't had any pie in over a year."

The economy is something like a water pump. If a pump loses its prime, you must pour water in it. The economy had to be primed in the Depression. There was no money in circulation. When President Roosevelt took office, he started various programs to "prime the pump." We had PWA, WPA, and CCC Camps to put a little money into the economy to get it started. PWA paid the workers about seventy-five cents per day. But, that was pretty good money back then. Boys could go to CCC Camps, stay in the barracks and the government would send thirty dollars per month to their families. PWA was for grown men, and they worked at repairing roads, cleaning out ditches, etc. Some of this was simply "make-work." I heard about one of those bosses who told his men, "We're out of shovels. You'll have to lean on each other!"

Another time, a farmer wanted to hire some PWA workers for hoeing cotton. So, the boss sent eight men over to the farm. The next day the farmer was asked if the workers had done okay. The farmer said, "They weren't too good. They worked in twos – two coming, two going, two shitting, and two hoeing."

But, these programs were not simply "hand outs". People had to show up for work, and some things like schools, auditoriums, etc. were built with these programs.

The economy began to pick up and things began to get better. Schools started back. In 1936, the Social Security Act was established. It was called the Old Age Pension and a song was written about it. I got the song off an old battery operated radio. We added some verses. Here is the song:

When that old age pension check comes to our door
Dear old grandma won't be lonesome any more
She'll be waiting at the gate
And every night she'll have a date
When that old age pension check comes to our door

These are some of the verses that we added:

When that old age pension check comes to our door
We won't have to worry any more
Every dog will have a bone
Every kid will have an ice cream cone
When that old age pension check comes to our door

When that old age pension check comes to our door
We don't have to worry any more
Though we're bent and gray
Good times will be here to stay
When that old age pension comes to our door

When that old age pension check comes to our door
I won't have to worry any more
I'll put the flapper on the shelf
And pick a grandma for myself
When that old age pension check comes to our door

There's a man who set this country upside down
With his old age pension rumor running around
So, if you want in on the fun
Send your dime to Washington
And the old age pension man will be around

At Christmas in 1930, my Dad said that we just wouldn't have anything for Christmas. But, my mother said that she was determined that we would have a coconut cake. She caught two hens and my brother and I carried them to the store and traded them for a coconut, some vanilla flavoring, and two pounds of sugar. Mother was able to make a delicious cake.

Things started to pick up, and they started the schools back. They paid the teachers with IOU's. They had changed the principal at the school near our home, and I could not get along with the new man. My brother was going to school at Cedar Bluff, Alabama. There was an old bus which we called a "chicken coop."

My brother rode that bus to school. I decided that I would go to school at Cedar Bluff too. The old bus didn't have any windows and dust and insects would get into our eyes. The bus was not in very good mechanical condition and one day it broke down. Some of the boys were sent to get something with which to make the repairs on the bus. Those of us who stayed at the bus got cold. We got some gasoline in a can and proceeded to build a fire. Someone kicked the can, and it landed on a girl's legs. All the other girls ran off, and this girl started to run also. I hollered to Bobby, "Don't let her run. She'll burn to death."

Bobby caught her. Velma pulled off her big winter coat and wrapped it around the girl's legs, thus smothering the fire. The girl had only one blister, just above the knee. We were lucky!

The bus had to cross a ferry going to Cedar Bluff. Twice a day we had to cross the Coosa River. All the students would get off the bus and walk down to the river bank. Then, after crossing the river on the ferry boat, they walked back up the river bank on the other side of the river. Going up and down the river bank was where all the fights would start. One ferryman liked to take a drink of whiskey. In the evening when we came by, the ferryman would be pretty "high", and the boys would man the boat. We had crossed so much that we could land the boat just as well as the ferryman could land it.

I went to Cedar Bluff School from the seventh grade. The outdoor toilet had commodes sitting on a concrete slab over a septic pit. One day I went down there, and a boy we called "Horsecollar" was calling, "Help! Help!" Horsecollar had fallen into the pit! I ran to get some help, and we fished him out of that predicament. Horsecollar stunk so bad that they had to carry him home in a box.

In chemistry class we kept a rabbit. I would slip into the classroom and let the rabbit out of his cage. He would run under the feet and between the legs of the girls in the class, and they would holler out. This would cause quite a commotion. I would say, "Well, I wonder how he got out of the cage."

We were preparing to do a chemistry experiment, and we were all warned to not put in too much sodium because it was likely to explode. There were some mean boys in the class, and I knew what they were going to do! They had an explosion and stunk up the room something awful. One boy fell back and hollered, "I'm blind!"

Someone said, "Well, open your eyes!"

When the thing exploded, a lid or something flew up and hit the ceiling. The boys left their mark on the school. The mark was still in the ceiling when the old school was torn down.

I bet some folks that I could climb the stairs and find my way into my classroom with my eyes shut. I found my way up the stairs, went into the classroom, and then noticed that everything was pretty quiet. I felt something that felt like wool. I opened my eyes and found that I had a hold on the Principal. He proceeded to chew me out pretty good.

My English teacher kept after everyone to buy a workbook. Dual Lindsey and I never bought one. We told her that we just couldn't afford one. I told her that my three sisters and I only got ten dollars a month to live on. One day I looked out the front door and there was Mrs. McCluney, my English teacher. She had come to see my parents to see if she could help buy me an English workbook. I ran to the back forty, but my folks caught up with me when I came home for supper.

One of my English teachers was killed in an automobile accident. We had a man teacher, Mr. Chapman, who was moved up to teach the English class. He loved humorous stories. He would make assignments for us to write themes and papers, and he wanted us to get up and read what we had written. I could not write. I'd get two pieces of paper and get up and act like I was reading them. The papers were blank! But, I never missed a lick. That was the only time I ever got a "B" on an English course. I never had to turn in the pages.

I finally got to graduate. But, if I hadn't dropped that Algebra class, I'd still be there!

We were set to have graduation. We were told that when we marched into the auditorium, one person would go to the left and the next person would go to the right. One guy asked, "Which is left?"

I laughed at him and said, "Do you mean that you are graduating from high school and don't know left from right?"

R. A. Tucker and I went in first and were sitting on the stage when the others came in. The teachers had told us not to swing our arms so one boy came in holding his arms out like he was walking a foot log. Calvin Tucker, a ninth grader, was to sing a solo. Someone let a young kid about two or three years old loose, and this kid was walking around and started pulling Calvin's leg. I tried to not laugh, but it was so funny. I don't recall what the speaker said, but I was grateful whenever he said something funny because it gave me an opportunity to laugh.

Chapter Two

PREWAR JOBS

We did not go to Florida after graduation the way they do now. I went back to the cotton patch. I graduated in 1939, and Hitler was making noise in Europe. Everyone figured a war was coming. In 1940, everyone had to take a blood test. We had never had a blood test, had never gone to the doctor. So, before we took the test, some of us figured that we needed to drink some wine to settle our nerves. We went to see a black man who sold wine. He took us down to the Bottoms where he kept the wine. When we got down there, he said that someone had stolen twenty dollars from him. He said one of us must have taken it. The truth of the matter is that he never had twenty dollars. But, he kept on and we finally put all our money together and paid the twenty dollars. We had to take the blood test without the wine, and it cost me seven dollars.

The law then was that we had to register for the draft. Everyone had an order number. My order number was 124. All of us were supposed to serve one year in either the Army or the Navy. In those days, everything was put in a song and one of the hits of the time was ***"I'LL BE BACK IN A YEAR, LITTLE DARLING."***

The words to that song were:

I'll be back in a year, little darling
Uncle Sam has called and I must go
I'll be back, don't you fear, little darling
You'll be proud of your soldier boy, I know
I'll do my best each day
For the good old U.S.A.
And we'll keep old glory waving high
Don't you worry and don't you cry

That one year turned out to be four and, in some cases, five years.

There weren't any jobs, so in 1940 I went down to the Draft Board and volunteered to go into the Service. I wanted to go ahead and get my year served. I was told that I would probably go in just before Christmas. I didn't want to go in just before the holiday. As it worked out, a man was caught bootlegging and was given the choice of going to prison or to the Army. That put off my entering the Army for a while.

My friend, Arthur Waddell, had a car and we buddied around quite a bit. Someone came down from Nashville looking to sign up people to attend an aircraft school, Anderson Aviation School. My buddy talked with the school representative and wanted to attend. They said that we could get a job after we finished that school. It sounded so good that I wanted to go too. I talked my Dad into paying for me to attend that school.

But, I had a problem. I'd volunteered to go into the Army. Therefore, before I signed up for the school, I went down and talked with the folks at the Draft Board. They said there were plenty of boys who were not doing anything and said I could go ahead and sign up for the school. So, I signed up to attend the aircraft construction school in Nashville, Tennessee.

I finished the course and still could not get a job. North American was starting up a plant in Texas. I had an aunt who lived in Texas, so I went there and applied for a job. I was told that Texas boys would get first preference in the jobs at that plant. I knew that I would not be getting a job in Texas. My sister, Peggy, lived in Oklahoma. So, I went there and worked in the wheat harvest for a while. I got a job driving an old model John Deere tractor. It did not have any power steering, and I'd have to stand up to turn the steering wheel. That job paid about two or three dollars a day. The pay was more than was being paid around home. People around Alexis were working for a dollar a day.

I worked there long enough to save up enough money to get home. I caught a bus on a Sunday morning and started traveling across country to home. In Mississippi, a big drunk guy sat down next to me. He went to sleep and got all over me. I elbowed him in the belly to make him stay on his side of the seat. If he had awakened, he probably would have killed me. But, I gave him a sore belly.

In Tuscaloosa, Alabama, a good-looking girl got on the bus and sat down next to me. She said that she was cold so I put my arm around her to help warm her. She propositioned me, but I didn't have any money. Afterwards, I always tried to carry some money, but I was never propositioned again.

I came home and told the Draft Board that I was ready to go into the Service. They planned to send a group in July, and I figured that I would be in that group. But, I wasn't. Glenn L. Martin had two plants and about three divisions in Baltimore,

Maryland. I wrote for an application, and I was hired through the mail. I had to get another release from the Draft Board. They told me to take the job in Maryland.

I went to Baltimore, Maryland. At the time, Baltimore was the fifth largest city in the United States. Frank Roe, Quinn Bouchillon, Dual Lindsey, and Robert Tidwell followed me to Baltimore and started to work for Martin also. We had a good group of Southern guys there.

There was a big old bar there that was called "The Monument House". Everybody would go there on the weekend and socialize. They sold beer, wine, and crab cakes. I had to carry my lunch to work in a paper sack. I got tired of Spam sandwiches and asked Miss Mack to make me a pineapple sandwich. Well, she had never heard of a pineapple sandwich. I told her to put some mayonnaise on bread and put in a slice of pineapple. Pretty soon, everyone was eating pineapple sandwiches.

Dual Lindsey and I were invited to a Polish wedding which lasted three days. I'd go to work, and they'd come pick us up to continue the celebration.

We moved uptown to a boarding house. There was a good looking girl who lived in the boarding house. Her name was Dorothy, but I called her "Dot". We both worked ten hours per day. She would come in after work and set the table for supper, and we would eat together. After supper, she would wash dishes, and I would dry them. Then, we'd go up to our rooms. At the top of the stairs, her room was on the right and mine was on the left. We'd go up the stairs together and smooch at the top before we went into our rooms. I bought her a ring, and we became engaged.

I received a letter from my Draft Board advising me that I'd been reclassified to 1A and would have to go into the Service. I would be given enough time for my company to hire a replacement for me. I went in and talked with my foreman. He told me that if I'd move my registration to Baltimore, he'd get me a deferment and I wouldn't have to go in at all. I asked him if he really had that much power. He told me that I needed to make up my mind whether I wanted to work there or go into the Army. I studied about it for three seconds and told him that I wanted to go into the Service.

Glenn L. Martin had hired some black women to bring into the work force. I think the company used me as a test to see how these new employees would be received. My foreman told me that they were bringing in a black. He didn't call her that. I won't say what he did call her. And he said he wanted me to teach her how to drive rivets. She came in and was a nice, sweet person. Pretty soon there were only two white boys, and the rest were blacks and/or women. This did not bother me. When I was growing up, we worked with blacks in the field. A black family lived close to us, and we'd go to their home on Sunday afternoon and sit around laughing and talking.

I bought a car while I worked in Baltimore. That was the first car I ever had. I had never even owned a bicycle before I bought that car. When I got ready to come home, Robert Tidwell, who was also working up there, said that he thought he'd go home too.

Chapter Three

BECOMING A MARINE

We got home and were supposed to report to Fort McClellan on February 15, 1943. Billy May had turned eighteen on February 7, 1943. Emmet Dake had been deferred for farming. They wanted to go into the Service. I suppose they wanted to get away from farming. Anyway, they went to the Draft Board and volunteered. That suited the Draft Board just fine. Three days later, they brought a letter to show me. I knew what it was and told them that sounded okay to me. I knew that now I would have to go into the Service myself.

When we arrived at the induction center, they asked if any of us had a high school diploma. There were thirty-eight men from Alabama. Three of us, Billy May, another guy, and I had graduated from high school.

I was going into the Army. But, the other guys wanted to go into the Navy. Alabama's quota was to send nineteen men to the Marines at Parris Island. They asked for volunteers and got one. They picked eleven at random. They knew that seven were coming from Cherokee County, which made the nineteen. We did not have a choice. We were put into the Marines. Our papers were stamped USMC (United States Marine Corps).

We were told to go down the hall and sit down. I said, "You reckon' they're going to put us in the Marines?"

A Navy corpsman came and asked us why we were sitting there. We told him that we'd been instructed to sit down. He went to find another corpsman. They came back, and the second corpsman looked at us and said, "Oh, those are our Marines. We're going to give them a special physical."

We were ordered to strip off all our clothes, and we were examined by several doctors. We stayed nude until afternoon. We were fed and then were examined by other doctors. A psychologist asked me, "Do you think you'll make a good soldier, sailor, or marine?"

I told him, "I figure I'll make as good as the next man."

We were told that all branches of service were open, and we could make a choice. We'd already agreed that we wanted the Navy so we all were given tags for that. We were sent home and told that we'd be called in about thirty days.

I went back to Baltimore to see my friends and my fiancé, Dot. When I returned, we'd been ordered to report to Birmingham on the fifteenth of March.

We caught the bus in Centre and had to change buses in Gadsden. The bus to Birmingham rolled up and about thirty people ran to board it. The other guys just about panicked. "What are we going to do?"

I said, "We're not going to do anything, just stand here."

The bus driver opened the door and said, "I have seven seats available and seven sailors waiting for them. Where are the sailors?"

I hollered, "Here we are!" We were on our way. I never knew how the bus driver knew how many sailors there were.

Alabama had to send nineteen Marines to Parris Island. We were to meet a bunch of boys from the Northeast. There were some from Massachusetts, Delaware, New Hampshire, Connecticut, and Maryland. And there was one from Virginia. We all made up a platoon that sometimes was called "T*he Platoon from Everywhere*."

When I arrived at the center, I said, "I have all our papers."

Some crabby officer shouted out, "Hand those papers to me!"

He muttered that if we had good eyesight and were in good health, we'd be Marines. Otherwise, we'd go into the Navy. He stamped my papers USMC. I was ignorant and didn't know what that meant. I thought that I'd made lieutenant or something. But, I looked around and all the other boys had their papers stamped USMC also, and I knew there was no promotion.

I didn't even know what a Marine was. In Baltimore, I'd seen a Marine in a sharp dress green uniform. I was impressed and thought that if I ever had a uniform, that's the kind I wanted. Little did I know that I was about to get one.

I told a corpsman, "I wanted to go into the Navy."

He said, "Well, you're in the Navy. The Infantry Navy!"

Each of us was given a tag. Then we checked into the Birmingham Tutwiler Hotel. We were disappointed and disgusted and did not know what the future held. We bought us a bottle and went out on the town.

Chapter Four

BOOT CAMP

The following morning we were picked up early and carried to a building. I was still half asleep when we arrived there. We signed a lot of papers, and then we were sworn in. We had breakfast after being sworn in. That afternoon, we were put on a train. The recruiter kept saying, "Good luck, fellows. You're going to need it!"

Boy, he probably never knew that he was telling the truth!

That night, somewhere in Augusta, Georgia, we were told that some cots were available in the American Legion building. We slept there for about four hours. The next morning we got up and caught the train for Beaufort, South Carolina. In Beaufort, we were to meet a train coming from the north. We met that train, and that's when the yelling began. We found out what Boot Camp was going to be like.

Some cattle trucks with high beds were brought around to the train station. They hollered and whooped and told us to get into the trucks. We got in and found ourselves packed in like sardines. We had to stand up and were packed in so tightly that we couldn't fall. We headed off for Parris Island.

We unloaded at Parris Island at lunchtime. They fed us chow. Afterwards, we got to go to the field and were organized into platoons. We were in Platoon 150. Then, we were carried to the Receiving Area. We were told to strip and give our clothes for shipment back home. They told us to take our underclothes and throw them into a garbage can. Since I had not known where I was going, I had worn a suit, white shirt, and a tie. I had on new underwear that I hated to throw in the trash.

We were all new. They put us in a barber chair. Zip, zip … they cut off every bit of our hair. I had pretty wavy hair and the barber said, "That would make some woman a pretty wig."

After the haircut, there was a guy with a brush. He supposedly would brush the hair off us, but he made sure that he hit everyone on the penis with that brush. Then we went into the shower. We pulled on a rope and water started coming out of the showerhead. As soon as I got in and pulled the rope, they began hollering, "Get out! Get out!"

I went down the hall, and a pair of dungarees hit me in the side of the head. They threw underwear at me, threw big brogan shoes, all the time yelling, "Get 'em on! Get 'em on!" They kept hollering, but we were working as fast as we could.

I estimate that within seven minutes, we had fallen out and were ready to go. In September of 2007, I visited Parris Island and was told that new recruits are now processed in seven DAYS. I told them that we had been processed in seven MINUTES.

We got out and lined up in ranks. We didn't know how to march, but they moved us to another place. They threw two blankets at us and then the sheets. If you weren't alert, they would knock you down when they threw stuff at you. Then they carried us into the barracks and showed us how to make up our "sacks." We had to learn the Marine name for things. The bed was called a "sack". They showed us how to make it up military style. They carried us to the PX to pick up towels, wash cloths, razors, toothbrushes and all those things.

The next morning, they carried us out and formed us into platoons. They would put the tallest ones on the end, and then come down with the next tallest and so until the shortest one was on the end. I didn't want to be the leader. I was the second (second tallest) from the end. That suited me fine because the first was the leader.

The Marines have a name for everything, and we had to learn those names. They don't have a toilet. They called the toilet the "Head." The floor was called the "deck," and the sides were called "bulkheads." The ceiling was called the "overhead." They gave us a little cap which they called a "piss-cutter." I liked that little cap okay, but I never knew the real name for the cap. From day one until this day, I have called it a "piss-cutter."

They carried us to the armory and issued a rifle, the MI Garand, to each of us. This rifle weighed sixteen pounds. We had to grasp the rifle six inches from the muzzle and carry it back to the barracks without allowing the butt to touch the ground. Holding the heavy rifle in such a manner got rough as we marched back to the barracks.

They gave us instructions on what was expected of us. We were asked to remember how we came in. We were told that if we made a Marine in ten weeks, we would go out the same way. If we did not make a Marine in those ten weeks, we would go out in a pine box!

I didn't want to go out in a pine box so I resolved then and there that I would do my best to make a Marine. We were issued a "Red Book." It was a military book and contained the eleven General Orders. Our sergeant said, "This is your Bible, and I am your God." He told us that if we kept our ears open and our mouths shut, we would be all right. If you did that, you made it pretty good.

We were issued a bucket and a brush which we placed under our bunks. We had to do our own washing. We would do our washing together and hang our clothes out to dry. We had to put a guard on the drying clothes because other outfits would steal them.

I slept on the top bunk. The boy who slept on the bunk under me was called my "butt-hole buddy."

They ran us around and hollered at us for about three days. I had not even had a chance to speak to the guys who went with me from Cherokee County. Billy May was about three bunks down from me, and I didn't even have time to speak to him. They would run us around, and we'd just fall into the bunk and sleep. Seems like we'd just lie down, and they'd get us back up again. About the third day, they gave us a ten minute break to go back into the barracks. I stepped out the back door and stood there mopping perspiration and remarked to some of the other guys, "I know why a Marine doesn't mind dying. It would be a pleasure to get out of this hell!"

But, we went along, learning a little each day. The Drill Instructor (DI) had a tough time with us because we didn't know anything. We did a lot of close-order drill, left face, right face, right shoulder arms, etc. We didn't know anything about that at all. I could march fairly well. I was a pretty good dancer and marching was a matter of rhythm and timing. If you could dance, you could do okay with the marching. But, I didn't know about column marching or flank marching. I had to learn all of that. Some of the boys were kind of clumsy. They couldn't dance, and it was hard for them to march. The DI would yell at them and tell them to get into step. There was a Dake boy who went with us, and he was a big, tall, clumsy fellow. He'd get out of step, and the DI would holler at him, "Dake, if you don't get in step, I'm going to come up there and we'll fight the Civil War again!"

Some of the boys were so big they couldn't get dungarees to fit them. Those guys were issued blue coveralls instead of dungarees. Consequently, those guys were called "Little Boy Blue." The DI would shout, "Little Boy Blue, if you don't get in step, I'm gonna come up there and kick your butt!"

We were learning more and becoming accustomed to military life. They would get us up at 3:00 a.m. each morning, and we'd start to work. We had to clean the barracks each day. Each squad had a particular job. My squad had to clean the bulkheads, and there wasn't much to keeping that clean. The squad that had to clean the deck had a much tougher job. They had to mop each day. After cleaning the barracks, we would fall out for running exercise. It would still be dark when we fell out. We would run for an hour. We would be strung out so that when we got down to the lower end, we could catch a breather for a few minutes. I did that because I knew that we had sixteen more hours ahead of us.

They opened the Mess Area for chow at 6:00. I never ate breakfast before going into the Service. I'd just get up and go to work. But, when I got to Parris Island, I could not get enough to eat. They ran us and worked us so much that I would eat everything I could get my hands on. One day, the Catholic boys observed some kind of religious holiday, and they asked me if I wanted their bacon. I wound up with a plate of bacon. I told them, "I don't wish any of you bad luck, but I wish you had a day like this every day."

After eating, we would take exercise. And after that, we would drill – close order drills. We'd drill just about all day. The DI would call us "stupid clowns", "jarheads", and other such names. They can't do that anymore. They can't call recruits names, and they can't put their hands on the recruits.

The Marine way for us to sign our names was last name first, first name last. One day, I forgot and signed my name the normal way. I realized my mistake and went to the sergeant and told him. He grabbed me by the collar and reamed me out. He called me "stupid" and every other name he could think of. Afterwards, I never made that mistake again. I kept my ears open, and my mouth shut.

In our outfit, there was a big boy from Cherokee County. We had gone into the Marines together. He had problems in marching and could never get into step. A teacher at Cedar Bluff High School, L. B. Sibert, had been in the Service. He had taught us to skip to get back into step. But, this guy did not know how to do it. When he tried, he would look like an old hound dog that was dragging his foot. He looked funny, and I would laugh. Another big, heavy-set guy in our outfit would fall down within a few yards whenever we had to "double time." I would laugh at that too.

There was a drill where the DI would order us outside the barracks. Then, he'd holler for us to get inside. Outside. Inside. Outside. Inside. The drill would go on for about twenty minutes. Some boys would be going out the door, and some would be trying to come in. I played football so I would lower my head like a fullback and go through the door. Sometimes, I'd take four or five guys back.

I had to go down one night and get a tooth pulled. The dentist gave me two shots, and I told him to wait because the tooth was not dead. He gave me two more shots, and it still hurt. At that point, he said that he was going to pull that damn tooth. When he pulled the tooth, I screamed. The dentist said, "Well, that wasn't too bad for a Marine!"

I believe that he must have injected water instead of Novocain because I never felt any effect from the shots he gave me.

About two weeks into our training, we were ordered to take a full pack march. First, we went to the dispensary, and each of us got two shots. Then we put our packs back on and picked up our rifles and started off. We didn't run, but we had to double time. We went down and performed a military operation, and then we started back to the base. I felt so tired that I thought I would fall out with the next step. Now, to fall out was a disgrace! I knew that the other guys were hurting just as much as I was. I had plowed a mule and those Yankee boys had never done that. A Marine just did not fall out. Just when I felt as if I could not take another step, someone (I don't know who) started singing the Marine Hymn. We went into the base singing. We went all the way to the barracks, marching and singing. Then, the DI came in and asked, "Are you tired?"

We shouted, "No, sir!"

Then he'd ask again. I don't know why he made us do like that because we were all exhausted. But, we found out that we could do more than we thought we could!

When I was growing up, I never drank any milk except buttermilk. I just did not like sweet milk. But, when we came off that hike, there was a tub of cold, sweet milk. I was exhausted and suffering from the effects of those shots we'd been given. I wanted something. That sweet milk was the best thing I have ever tasted.

We stayed constipated for about four days. But, there wasn't anything to worry about because the sergeants would work it out of us. Then, they fed us a bunch of beans. I had a bowel movement, and I suppose the others did also.

We had a parade. We were in one of the older, more experienced platoons. So, they had us lined up to be on the outside, nearest the reviewing stand. There was a new platoon on the inside, away from the reviewing stand. Somehow, someone panicked and there was a stampede. Everybody got all mixed up. The parade was cut short. We never went past the reviewing stand. After our platoon got straightened out, they asked if everyone was present. Someone said, "No, LaPiere is missing!"

We finally found him. He had got mixed in with another platoon and just stayed there. Boy, this fellow was really chewed out. I could feel sorry for LaPiere because I had got in with another group myself. But, I had sense enough to realize my mistake, and I ran and got back with my platoon.

We had a sergeant, Sgt. Clark. I liked him okay, but he could raise more hell in ten minutes than anyone else could in a day. We had a PFC Russell. He was a rebel from South Carolina, and he wasn't too hard on us. We had a PFC Burnham, and we had a corporal whose name I cannot recall. The time we had in the barracks was about the only time we could relax. The DI stayed in the barracks, and a corporal often visited him. Whenever he came into the barracks, the first one who saw him was supposed to shout, "Attention!"

All the other guys had to jump to the end of the bunks and stand at attention.

One night, this corporal came in, and my butt-hole buddy was writing a letter to his girlfriend. He was slow getting to the end of his bunk. The corporal chewed him out and reached under the bunk and placed a pail over my buddy's head. Then he ordered him to shout "ATTENTION" while wearing that pail. I laughed.

The corporal turned to me and asked if I thought it was funny?

I said, "No, sir."

But, it was funny to see him standing there shouting while he had a bucket on his head. The fellow earned his nickname that night and was called "Bucket head" from then on.

The corporal said that I laughed in the ranks a lot.

I said, "no, sir."

Actually, I did laugh in the ranks a lot. A lot of the stuff seemed funny to me.

We were sort of self-disciplined. If a Marine messed up, the group would have to put in extra time. Therefore, we'd put pressure on each other to do things the right way. Of course, we were not allowed to fight. But, if someone continued to mess up and caused all of us to have to put in extra work, when the lights went out he might fall over a foot locker or something. When sixty-nine men tell you to shape up, you'll shape up.

As a joke, I walked in one night and shouted, "Attention."

Everybody jumped up and I said, "That's okay. It's just Godfrey."

The second time I did that, I was told to cut it out. The guys said that we had enough of that junk without me doing it too. I never pulled that stunt again!

We had one guy in the platoon who was always very fidgety. He just could not be still in the ranks. A lot of time, the person behind him would kick him to make him shape up. The kid's name was Murray. One day, Murray came up missing. We finally found him in the barracks. He had slipped back into the barracks and had gone to sleep. They found out that this kid had enlisted in the Marines when he was only fifteen years old. The reason he could not be still was that he was just a kid. They let him stay in the Marines.

Every afternoon we had to water the lawn. Actually, we did not have a lawn. It was only sand. But, we'd all get a bucket of water, pour it on the sand and then smooth it out. We had an older guy in the platoon, and one day he decided that he would write a letter and not carry water. We all told everybody to get an extra bucket of water. Then we dragged him out. We almost drowned the guy by throwing sixty-eight buckets of water on him. Then, we rolled him in the sand. He looked like a mud man. The next day this guy was the first one out with his bucket. This is sort of how we disciplined each other. I don't remember the man's name.

In the military, we had to say "sir" to everything. That didn't bother the Southern boys because we were taught to say "yes, sir" and "no, sir" as well as "yes ma'am" and "no ma'am." But the boys from the North had not been taught this way, and they had some problems in saying "sir" to everything. You could see in one boy's eyes that he resented having to follow orders. The sergeant got on him pretty bad about his attitude. Finally, the boy said, "Sir, I haven't said anything."

The sergeant replied, "Yeah, but I know what you're thinking."

We were carried to a swampy area and were told that we had to cross quicksand. We were told that every time they go through this exercise, two or three men are lost. I did not know if that was true or not. But, I didn't want to get stuck in quicksand. I went across with mud and water spraying ten feet on either side of me. Then, we had to go back and wash our clothes.

Now, the Marines have laundry service. We also had Mess Duty, had to do our own cooking. Now, they have private food companies supplying food to the troops.

Someone stole my poncho. We fell out one morning in the rain and fog. Sgt. Clark asked me where my poncho was. I told him that someone had lifted it.

He said, "You'd better get one! Understand?"

I said, "Yes, sir."

The whole platoon set out to acquire a poncho for me. The poncho is rolled up and tied with two strings and then hung on the cartridge belt in the back.

We had to go in and view a movie. Some of the Boots in the movie house would go to sleep. One of my buddies was to cut a poncho off the belt of the Boot sleeping in front of him. But, my buddy's knife was so dull that he woke the guy. We put on our packs, got our rifles and went to the rifle range. When we got there, we found that someone had left a poncho. The Range Officer asked, "Who does this poncho belong to?" My whole platoon said, "It belongs to Godfrey."

On the rifle range, we had a lot of free time. This is where we really bonded with everyone. Boys from the north got to know the southern boys. I really liked the northern boys. I was always the clown of the group, and these guys would laugh at my old jokes. I told them about a bus robbery.

> A robber got on a bus and announced that he intended to rob all the men and kiss all the women. The driver told the robber, "look here, you may rob the men, but you can't kiss our women!"

An overweight old maid stood up in the rear of the bus and said, "Driver, you shut up! There's a real man robbing this bus."

Another one:

A robber was on a bus and came to an old maid. She said that she did not have any money. The robber said that he would have to search her just to make sure. So, he searched her and she was squirming around all the while. Finally, the robber said, "You were telling the truth. You don't have any money."

The old maid said, "No, I don't. But, if you'll search me again, I'll write you a check."

Others:

I went into a restaurant and asked the waitress if she had frog legs. She said, "No, arthritis makes me walk this way." I ordered eggs. When they were served, they didn't look too good. I asked the waitress if the eggs were fresh, and she said, "Certainly, I just laid them today."

She asked where I was from. I told her Lickskillet, Alabama, where chicken tastes like chicken, and girls don't smell like talcum powder. We had two windmills but we didn't have enough wind so we took one of them down. We had a black pig that we called ink. Every time we put him in a pen, he ran out.

We spent some leisure time on the rifle range. But, then some of the guys had to go swim. Some could not swim. Billy May had never learned to swim. Those who could not swim were called "Ducks." Their DI would make them count cadence by quacking. They would walk by saying, "I am a duck. I will learn to swim. Quack, quack."

On the rifle range, we lived in Quonset huts, twelve men per hut. In our hut, there was a man named Carriba who was from Falls River, Massachusetts. He always hung around us in the barracks, and he wound up in the Quonset hut with us. He told me what a recruiter had told him. He said that he was warned to avoid the Southern boys because they would sooner cut your guts out as to look at you. I said, "Oh, so that is the reason you hang around the Southern boys."

Sometimes the boys would ask me to play sergeant. They would volunteer to march, and I'd play like Sgt. Clark. I'd ask one of the southern boys where he was from and he'd answer, "Bauston, Massachusetts." Or the northern boys would drawl, "I'm from Alaabaamaa."

One night, I slipped out and got the boys in my hut some ice cream. I got cups, not cones. We weren't allowed to have anything like that. We weren't even allowed to go to the PX.

On the range, we were left pretty much alone. PFC Russell would check on us occasionally, but he didn't bother us. The other PFC would just get us to the firing range and leave us alone.

If you could hold the rifle steady and squeeze the trigger, the guys on the range could get you on target. If, for instance, you were constantly to the left of the bull's eye, they would tell you to put so many clicks of right windage, and you would be on target. But, if you were all over the target, they didn't know what to tell you, and they could not help you.

We would march to the firing range in columns of two because we marched on the sidewalk. A column of seventy men would be stretched out pretty far. I liked to be in the back so that I could laugh and clown around. One day, PFC Russell was to march us to the range. I was sure he would give a "right face" command, so I lined up on the left. Instead, he gave a "left-face" command. This put me in the front of the column. I thought that, since I was in the front, I'd show these guys how to march. I was really strutting along. I was so sure that we were going to Range A that I did not listen to Russell's commands. He ordered "column right" and I turned left. I looked back, and no one was following. I had to run to catch up. PFC Russell said, "Damn, Godfrey! Don't you know right from left?"

All the guys got a kick out of that and kidded me quite a lot about it.

On the range, we would often be put behind the targets. We'd be in a pen known as the "butts". When a shooter would fire, we'd pull the target down, put a spotter on it and put it back up. Then, when it was scored, we'd pull the target down, put a patch over the bullet hole and put the target back up. This got to be a lot of work. And, our bunch seemed to get more target work than other groups. One thing that may have contributed to our getting target work is that we were proficient at handling the targets. When a group fired for record, work in the pits was really hard. The range officers would holler, "Get 'em down! Patch 'em! Get 'em up!"

We were pulling targets on the carbine range. There were two guys from Officer's Candidate School in the pits observing us work the targets. My buddy and I acted as if we did not know how to pull the targets. The two OCS guys proceeded to show us how to do it. The two prospective officers wound up doing all the work. We worked in the "butts", and they did the same.

If we worked in the "butts" on Record Day, we got extra credit. On Record Day, it got pretty tough. This was timed fire, and we had to hurry with the targets. The shooter would fire at the target; we'd lower it and place a spotter so that he could see where the bullet hit. Then, we'd lower the target, patch the hole and put it back up. If the shooter missed the target completely, we would wave a red rag on a stick. That was called "Maggie's drawers."

We fired from 200 yards, 300 yards and 500 yards. Each shooter had an individual coach who stayed with him all the way through the course. He would not holler at you. He was there to help you. If a boy could not get into position, the coach would sometimes step or sit on him to help him get down. I didn't have any problem in getting into position. But when I got into the prone position, my right elbow would slip out. I could not make my elbow stay where my coach told me to put it. Finally, he said, "Well, you're hitting the target so don't worry about it."

On Preliminary Day, we would go through the routine just as we expected to do on Record Day. On Preliminary Day, I shot

318 out of a possible 330. That was a "High Expert" score. Of course, on that day there was no pressure on me. But on Record Day, the pressure was on, and I only shot 304. I needed to score 308 to qualify as "Expert".

We would shoot prone, kneeling, sitting and offhand (standing). I was shooting slow fire sitting, at the 500 yard target. I was hitting the target, but the bullets were hitting almost off the black on the right side. My coach must have thought I was going to get off the target so he yelled for me to put in two clicks of left windage. I was excited and moved the sights two clicks of right windage. My next bullet landed way out, almost off target. My coach hollered, "Godfrey! What happened?"

He came over and checked and told me that I had moved the sights the wrong way. He put the weapon as it had been previously, and I continued firing. But, I had enough points to have made "Expert" if I hadn't messed up.

Next, we moved to the 300 yard target. This was rapid fire. We had to shoot, change clips, and continue firing. And, all this had to be done within just a few seconds. We would get on the firing line and the Range Officer would say, "Ready on the left! Ready on the right! Commence firing!"

Then, we had to drop down into the kneeling position. I did not drop exactly right, and I was not very steady. After firing, my coach asked how I did, and I said that I'd splattered them all over the target. When my target was brought to us, we found that the holes were spotted all over. My coach said, "You really did splatter that one."

We had to learn to squeeze the trigger. If the trigger was pulled, the rifle would be jerked off the target. On rapid fire, the shooter had to breathe between shots. If he did not, the breathing would throw his shot off.

We had to be careful on the range. One day I was shooting in the offhand position at a 200 yard target. Before I got a shot off, the target was pulled down. It came back up, and I had a bull's eye! I said, "That shot wasn't mine."

Someone else had shot my target. And, of course, that person got a "Maggie's drawers" for his shot.

One day, we were shooting rapid fire. We had to shoot and then change the clip. We were told when to lower the targets. One guy had a round left, and he fired as the target was going down. The sergeant said, "Who fired that shot? Who do you think you are? Sergeant York!"

Some of the guys did not qualify. It was just about a disgrace for a Marine to fail to qualify with a rifle. I didn't have any problems. I really wanted to qualify as an "Expert." But, I guess we were happy with what we did.

While we were loafing around, I told the guys about my first job in a dry goods store. One day a lady came in and said, "Young man, I'd like to see your underwear."

I said, "Ma'am, it's too hot. I'm not wearing any."

The next day, we had mess duty. When we were on the rifle range, each squad had one week of mess duty. That was the hardest work I had ever done – or have ever done since. We worked from 3:00 in the morning until 9:00 at night. I was glad when that week was finally over, and we returned to the main base.

Finally, we threw our sea bags onto the trucks, and we marched all the way to the main base. Sgt. Clark said that we'd got salty on the rifle range, and that he would take that salt out of us. You can bet that he did just that! In the morning, we would run before daylight. Then we would go to the mess hall for chow, and afterward we would go back out for exercise. By this time, we were getting pretty tough. We were Marines, and we could take it!

We were carried out to the boxing ring. One of us would be selected, and then someone else would be picked to box against that person. One day, a big old boy named Dake, who had come from Cherokee County with me, was selected. Then a guy named Berkowitz was picked to fight against Dake. Berkowitz had some experience at boxing. He would hit Dake, and Dake would go down. I wanted to tell Dake to stay down, but I was not allowed to say anything. Dake would come crawling back up, and Berkowitz would hit him again. I would be thinking to myself, "Stay down!" But, Dake would get back up. Berkowitz must have knocked Dake down at least three times before the fight was stopped.

One day I was standing around with nothing to do, and I had my hands in my pockets. A Drill Instructor, not our DI, came by and told me to get my hands out of my pockets. He then filled my pocket with sand. I thought I never would get all that sand out of my pocket. My locker keys were in the pocket and sand got all over them.

Occasionally, we would have inspection in the mornings. One morning our DI must have been in a very bad mood. As he moved through the ranks, a Boot would come to Port Arms and present his weapon for inspection. The DI would check it and say, "Write 1000 times, 'I must keep my rifle clean'."

He was saying this to everyone in the platoon. I just knew that he'd be dissatisfied with mine because he hadn't liked anybody else's rifle. But, about the time he got to me, a car with some girls came by. The DI looked around, looked back and said, "Godfrey, your rifle looks pretty good. You don't have to write."

Then he proceeded to inspect the others and went back to making them write. Out of the whole platoon, only two of us did not have to write, "I will keep my rifle clean." Of course, I ragged the other guys about this. I had to enjoy it while I could.

One day, Billy May had his rifle checked, and it was found to be dirty. Billy was carried to the captain.

Sometimes an officer or DI would walk up to us and ask, "What is the ninth (or any other number) General Order?"

We had to know the General Orders by number and be able to recite them when asked. Sometimes we'd be asked, "What happens when you pull the trigger?"

We would have to explain the workings of the rifle. I never had any problems with any of that. Most of us didn't.

One morning, we had inspection and Sgt. Clark came up to me. I came to Port Arms and he looked at me and said, "Godfrey, you look like a man with no arms and legs in a barrel of shit."

I don't know how a man in such a condition would look!

As we approached the end of our ten weeks of Boot Camp, we were feeling pretty good about ourselves. One day we had a parade. We were marching and looking pretty sharp. The band was playing, and we stopped at the viewing stand and did Port Arms. I was standing there with my mind a thousand miles away, thinking about my furlough and about seeing my girl. Suddenly, I heard them cussing a recruit, saying, "Look at that stupid guy. He's still at Port Arms!"

The band had finished the tune it was playing and had started playing the National Anthem. At that point, we were to Present Arms. I looked around and realized that the stupid guy they were talking about was me! But, it just so happened that whoever had spotted me was not my sergeant. So, I got by that time.

On the day before we finished our training, we were presented a Marine emblem. You are not a Marine until you get that emblem. We put on our emblems, and then went out for drill. They worked us pretty good. Then they chewed us out and told us that we were not worthy of being Marines. Some of the guys took off their emblems. I left mine on because I felt like I had worked for it and deserved it.

The next day, we got our khaki clothes out of the sea bags and got dressed for inspection. We didn't look too good because our khakis were wrinkled. Then our assignments were read. Up to that point, we had no idea where we would go or what we would do. Of the seven boys from Cherokee County, there were now only six. Kelly could not stand the pressure and did not make it. Some people just cannot stand pressure and will break down. That left six of us.

Dake, Hawthorne, Johnson, and Black were sent to the Fleet Marine Force as riflemen. Billy May and I were assigned to Cherry Point.

We had about a day to lie around and watch others come in. The next day, they got us up about 3:00 a.m. and got us out to the truck. Sgt. Clark was out there, and he came around and shook the hand of each man. For the first time, he told us that we were good men and good Marines. He said that he would not mind fighting with us any day.

It made me kind of sad to leave him after he bragged on me like that.

Chapter Five

STATESIDE DUTY

Before we left Parris Island, they gave us dress uniforms. They gave us what they thought would fit. We got dressed and got on a stage to be checked out to insure that the uniforms fit. You never saw a Marine who did not look sharp. A tailor was there to make alterations if a uniform could not be found to fit us.

They carried us to Beaufort where there were two trains awaiting us. One train was bound for Camp LeJeune, and the other was headed for Cherry Point. The boys who were headed to LeJeune were finally put into the Sixth Division, Twenty-ninth Marines. This was the only division formed outside the United States. That division was formed in Guadalcanal.

Billy May and I went to Cherry Point on an old World War I train. The cars had straight back seats. We ran out of water. As the train would go through the swamps, it would stop at the little towns. When the train stopped, little black boys would come out and dance for tips. They wanted us to pitch coins at them. One of the boys had a head for business. He bought two candy bars for a nickel each and sold them for a dime each. He didn't know it, but he probably could have gotten a quarter for each bar. We had not been paid all the time we were in Boot Camp, and only got paid when we shipped out. We didn't need any money in Boot Camp because we weren't going anywhere.

We rode all day to Cherry Point. We had been issued two blankets. I kept mine all the way through. I still have them. I brought them home with me. We had no linens. We just put one blanket on the mattress and covered ourselves with the other blanket.

Before we got assignments in Cherry Point, we were given a ten-day furlough. We caught a bus to Raleigh, North Carolina. When we arrived there, all the trains were running over with people. An old salty conductor told us that he did not have room for us. An MP intervened and told the conductor to let us on the train. He said, "These boys have got to go home!"

The conductor said that he had a family car in which we could ride. He then asked the MP if he was going with us. The MP replied that he was not going. That gave me a tip as to what to expect.

When we got into the family coach, we saw two civilian boys in two seats. Each was lying across the seat, occupying the space for two people. I told my buddy to take one of the civilians and I would take the other. We got them by the shoulders and told them that they had to sit up. We sat down comfortably in an air-conditioned coach. All the other coaches were hot, and people were standing.

Before long, some of the other Marines began looking for us and found us in that coach. Soon, the coach was filled with

Marines. There were some girls in the coach. They had been to Quantico.

I went to Baltimore. I had to go see my girl. I told Dot to get ready, that I wanted her to go to Alabama with me. After a couple of days, we started to Alabama. We rode a train all night and arrived in Atlanta. There we had to change trains to go to Rome, Georgia. The train from Atlanta to Rome was so crowded that we had to stand between coaches. Our faces were black from smoke and cinders. I called home, and my parents sent someone to Rome to give us a ride to Alexis.

We spent some time at home in Alexis. We did not spend the full ten days at home because I had spent time in Maryland.

When it was time to go back to camp, Billy May decided to go with us. He had another day remaining on his furlough, but since he didn't want to travel alone, he gave up that day. We caught the train from Rome to Atlanta, and then Billy and I had to change trains to go to Cherry Point, North Carolina. I kissed my girl goodbye in Atlanta, and that is the last time I ever saw her.

We proceeded to Cherry Point and found that we still had not been assigned. We were put in a barracks where we still did not have any linen. We were put to work on the second shift. Our job was scraping paint off a C-47 airplane.

We worked for about a week, and then we were called down for assignment. I had worked in an airplane factory, and the guy in charge said that I should go to the Aircraft Repair (AR) shop where they repair planes. The sergeant said that he had plenty of men, but if I stayed there as a guard I could move into the AR barracks. I did not do that. If I had known that Billy May had been assigned there, I might have stayed.

When the Marines need men, they put you where you are needed. The sergeant told me that I probably would be put into General Duty and there was no telling where I'd go. I said, "Well, I think I'll take that chance."

But, everything worked out okay.

I was sent to Oak Grove, not too far from Cherry Point. Oak Grove was a little old air field that had previously been a tobacco field. A river flowed through the place. The field was very small, but big enough for planes to take off and land. There was a hedgerow on one side of the field. We would hide in that hedgerow because if we were caught being idle, we would be put to work washing windows or something to keep us busy.

Soon, we received orders to prepare to go to France. They wanted our planes. Corsairs could carry rockets, and they were needed to blow up German rocket bases in Southern France. We were excited about that, and we began working day and night, packing stuff in preparation to be shipped out.

One time, I was at a table saw filling orders for 2x4's, etc. I had been there so long that a sergeant became worried that I would fall into the saw. He told me to go home and get into the sack. I did that and got up the next morning and got right back at the job. Every morning we would put what we had boxed the previous day and load it onto a C-47. That plane was then flown to Norfolk, Virginia. We crated all the stuff we would need. They had issued us rifles, bayonets, shovels – whatever we would need for combat.

About two days after we had everything ready, our orders were cancelled. The folks in charge did not know what to do with us after the orders were cancelled.

I had been out on liberty one night and when I returned, I found that a bunch of us had been put on Mess Duty at Officers' Mess. A Marine had to have thirty days of duty to serve at Officers' Mess. I went down to the Officers' Mess and sat down outside. I dozed off to sleep. A sergeant came out and said that he needed someone for pots and pans. That is the worst job there is.

Someone said, "How about getting that guy that is asleep down there?"

Well, that was me. That was a terrible job, and I stayed on it for about two weeks. I told myself that I had to get off this job. I lathered my hands with strong scouring soap and put them into water that was as hot as I could stand. I did this until my hands looked terrible, almost bleeding. I was determined to get off that job.

I went to the sergeant and showed him my hands. He took me off pots and pans and put me on garbage detail. That was a good deal. All we had to do was set the garbage cans out before each meal, empty them, and wash them afterwards. We could go to the food locker during the day. If we got hungry, we got our mops as if we were going to mop up in there. Then, we'd find whatever we wanted to eat.

The old mess sergeant was a Greek. One day, he got some apricots that he planned to serve to the officers. He came in and found us eating them. We were eating apricots, the cooks were eating apricots, and when it was time to serve the officers, there were no apricots!

We would tell the boys who were working as waiters, "Don't give all the ice cream away."

If there was any left, we ate it. Pretty soon, if an officer asked for more ice cream, he would be told that there was no more. That way, we would have more ice cream for ourselves.

One night one of the guys had stolen a gallon can of fruit cocktail intended for the Officers' Mess. We used a fire bottle to cool it with because it had ice in it. After that he opened the can with a knife, but we had nothing to eat with. So, the guys just stuck their hands down in the can to get a handful of fruit cocktail. Marines can do some crazy things.

An Indian cannot hold alcohol. One night an Indian boy got high on beer. He was throwing rocks and things at the barracks. He had us pinned down, and we had to call the MP's to come get him.

We got the word that we were going to be sent to California. I got my gear and loaded it onto a truck. I was carrying a rifle, a bayonet, and a shovel – ready to go into combat. I was weighted down with so much stuff that I had to be helped off the truck.

We got on a train and went south all night. We didn't know where we were going. I was on guard duty and was in the mail car from 4:00 a.m. until 6:00 a.m. The train stopped, and I saw someone standing in the rail yard. I hollered, "Where are we?"

He told me that we were in Waycross, Georgia.

We proceeded to Montgomery, Alabama. Some of the guys wanted to know how far it was to my home. I told them that I guessed it to be about 90 miles.

We passed through Mobile and on to Dallas/Fort Worth, Texas. Most of the trip, we stayed in Texas. We got in a field and took some exercises there.

We finally got out of Texas. About a day and a half later, we had to go down a mountain. I think the engineer of that train must have been drunk. He scared the daylights out of me. He would put on the brakes, and then we'd hit the curve and all of us would be tossed from side to side. I had got a plate of food with a peach on it. I wanted to save my peach, but it would run up and down my sleeve.

We finally went to California, and we moved into the Mojave Desert. We stopped at a little town there.

When you come to the desert from the East, your nose begins to dry out. The air is so dry that your nostrils will dry, and you feel as if you need to blow your nose. When you blow your nose, it begins to bleed like a stuck hog. After we'd been in Mojave for about four days, they came down and said that our outfit needed to furnish an MP for that night. They asked if anyone could shoot a .45?

All the guys said, "Yeah! Godfrey can shoot the eyes out of anything! He's from Texas."

I tried to tell them that I didn't know how to shoot a pistol, but I was told that I was the MP and I had a .45 and an MP armband. When I was outfitted with the pistol and armband, I told them, "We'll not have any shooting tonight!"

When I got down to the club, I was standing around and a lady Marine captain sent word for me to come see her. She was in charge of the club and asked me if anyone had told me what my duties would be.

She said, "Well, I'll tell you. You are to stand around and not allow anyone with sleeves rolled up to enter. Make them keep their tables clean and make them behave."

There were to be officers as well as enlisted men there. I was given a billy club, and I walked around and occasionally hit it on a table and say, "Clean it up."

After a while, my nose began to itch. I blew my nose, and it began to bleed. I went outside and tried to stop the nosebleed. Somehow, I got blood on my uniform and club.

The place closed at 10:00, and I went back to turn in my pistol, armband, and billy club. Somebody noticed the blood and said, "Man, what happened?"

I just said, "That was a tough bunch down there."

We stayed in the desert from August until February 1st, and I think it rained one time while we were there. But, we had dust storms. Those storms would pick up sand and hit you in the face and eyes, especially at night while you were on guard duty.

Bricks were used to build the barracks. The wind would blow down anything other than bricks. When we had a dust storm, I'd awake the next morning and I could see a white spot where I had laid. The dust got into the barracks and my sack somehow.

I learned some more of the Marine language. One of the phrases was for toast covered with gravy and chipped beef. We called it "shit on a shingle" or SOS. That was a new term for me. Pinto beans were called "thirty-eights."

The desert was cold at night. When I had guard duty from 2:00 a.m. until 4:00 a.m., I would put on all the clothes that I could find. There was no way anyone could slip up on us in that desert so I would holler over at the guy on the next post, and we'd meet halfway and talk.

For a while, I had guard duty on the main gate. That was pretty good duty. We kept a rag, and if someone was going on liberty with dusty shoes, we would make him wipe his shoes before we'd let him out. We didn't want anyone out who did not look sharp.

One time, I had duty with a sergeant. We were on from 8:00 a.m. until 12:00 p.m. Anyone coming through the gate with a bottle was required to put a little into a cup which the sergeant kept there. By the time my duty ended, I was feeling no pain.

One time I was on guard duty at the PX. There was a dog that hung around the place. There were dogs all over the base, but this one stayed around the PX. If there was any traffic or activity going on, the dog was alert. But if everything got quiet, I'd be standing guard, and the dog would stretch out and start snoring. I told him that he ought to let me sleep, and he should stay awake.

The nearest town to our base was Bakersfield, California. It was a good serviceman's town. Bakersfield was great. We'd have to go over a mountain to get to Bakersfield, and there was a small town on top of the mountain. This town was called Tahatchkee. One day, I was exploring around that little place and found a pool of water that was so pretty and inviting that I decided to take off my uniform and go "skinny-dipping." I was having a lot of fun when I glanced up and found myself looking at a woman who had the meanest appearance that I had ever seen. She was big and looked as if she could be on the mud-wrestling team at UCLA.

She asked me if I could read. I assured her that I could read, and I told her that if she would leave, I'd come right out. She said that she was not going to leave. I said, "Then turn around until I can get my clothes back on."

She refused to do that. I was getting pretty cold, so I felt around and found a dish pan lying on the bottom of the pool. I held the pan in front of me and got out of the pool. I apologized to the woman and told her that I knew what she must be thinking about me. She said, "Yeah. And, I know what you're thinking. You are thinking that pan has got a bottom in it."

My buddy, Holcomb, and I had a couple of girls in Bakersfield. Their names were Betty and Susan, but the Marines name everything so we called one of them "cow" and the other we called "rabbit." I went with the cow. We called her the "cow" because she had big boobies. The rabbit had teeth that stuck out. We dated these two girls some.

There was a big barn dance, a square dance, on Saturday nights. I went there practically every Saturday night and just about everyone there knew me. I'd speak to them and carry on small talk. The folks there would not let me pay for anything.

I met a girl there whose name was Nickie. When Holcomb got back to the base, he made fun of her. He said, "When Nickie was born, she had no mouth. Her parents told the doctors to make her a mouth 'from here to here'. The doctors misunderstood and thought they had said 'from ear to ear'. That's why she is all mouth."

I told Holcomb, "Now, you quit talking about the girl I love."

We could catch a train to Bakersfield if we had the fare which was $1.50. One night Holcomb and I caught the train. The best seats were always saved for any civilians who happened to be riding the train. I had figured out how things worked. On this night, there was a rope at the end of our car. I told Holcomb to follow me, and I just stepped over the rope.

When we got to the next car, we noticed that the passengers were chained together. It was a prison car, and these folks were being carried to prison. There were two guards with them, and the guards told us that it was okay for us to sit down. We sat down and started a conversation with the guards. We noticed that the guards appeared to have no weapons. We asked them where they kept their guns. We were told that the guns were concealed but were available if needed. The prisoners in each seat were chained together, two by two. When they got up to go to the bathroom, the guards told them, "You'll have to get into step."

One of the prisoners was a bald guy who they said had killed his wife. He was scheduled to be executed. This bald guy wanted to play poker with us. I told him, "No way!" Where you're going you won't need money, and I don't want to play with someone who has nothing to lose."

We rode all the way to Bakersfield with the prisoners. When we got up to leave the coach, I suppose that the people around the train thought that two Marines were being carried to prison.

Another time, at Christmas, half the base personnel were to be given liberty for Christmas and the other half would be off for New Year. My buddies and I chose to be off for Christmas. We each got a seventy-two hour pass. We got out on the highway early in the morning. The highway was lined with Marines wanting to catch a ride to Bakersfield. I said, "We won't ever be able to get a ride with all these guys along."

So, four of us tied four packs of cigarettes together and as a car would come by, we'd wave the cigarettes at the driver. The second car that came along stopped. The driver said, "My car is just about loaded, but get in. I've got to have those cigarettes!" So, we caught a ride to Bakersfield.

We went skating that night. I could skate. But, I would fall for meanness, knock people down and generally act a fool. The people who ran the skating rink blew the whistle at me, and I think they wanted to ask me to leave. But they were probably afraid I would refuse.

On Saturday night, the four of us split up and went to different places. I went to the barn dance, and the others went to other places. When I came into the motel later, I was kidding the other guys. They told me to shut up, but I went right along kidding them. The three of them threw me out of the motel room, and I was wearing only my shorts.

There I stood in just my underwear with a man and a woman coming down the hall. In those days, we just did not show ourselves in underwear. We just didn't do that. I tried to hide in the shadows, and finally told the guys to just let me in long enough to get my clothes and money, and I would go elsewhere. They let me in and gave me back, if I recall, a dollar and a half. I went down to the lobby of the motel and slept on a couch there. I often did that. I'd take off my shoes. I'd take off my field blouse and scarf, use those for cover and go to sleep. Every morning when I awoke there would be a blanket over me. I never said anything. But, I reckon the night clerk would put a blanket over me.

The USO in Bakersfield had said a family wanted to feed the boys Christmas dinner. Cavendish, DeMere and I signed up for it. We were chowhounds anyway, and on Christmas morning, the man came and picked us up and carried us to his home.

We were playing a game of badminton, and a pretty girl came by riding a horse. I ran and jumped on the horse behind her. My buddies thought that was really something! She rode me around for a short while, and then carried me back to my buddies.

One of my friends was from Massachusetts, and I don't think he had ever seen a horse. Certainly, he had never ridden one. Finally, I got him to climb on the horse. He wanted to get on backwards, but I told him the correct way to do it. I got him on the horse, and he told the horse, "Let's go."

The horse just stood there. I told him, "You've got to cluck to him."

He said, "What do you mean?"

I showed him how to cluck to the horse and make it go. He said, "You southern boys even know how to speak the same language the horse understands."

It was quite comical to see him on that horse.

When we went into dinner, the head of the family was seated at the head of the table. He carved the turkey, and we passed our plates to him. I wanted some white meat so I told him, "On the base, I always get the landing gear. Could you give me some white meat, please?"

I got what I wanted.

Some of the family members commented that it was odd that a boy from Alabama was with boys from Ohio and Massachusetts. I said, "Well, I had to show them the way up here."

We ate dinner, and the lady there told us that if we had dates, we could go. We didn't have dates so we stayed there until dark. She played the piano, and we sang Christmas carols. She didn't feed us supper, but she gave us another piece of pie. We had Christmas with a good family. It was almost like having Christmas at home.

Holcomb and I volunteered to work in the laundry. We were sent over there one day, and we started talking to the ladies who worked there. We asked if we could get a job there, and one of the ladies said that she knew the captain and was sure she could get us moved. The reason we wanted to work there was that we could get liberty every weekend. They worked the house out of us. We were not allowed to work together. Each one of us had to work with one of the women, and they enjoyed bossing us around. But, we could get off on the weekend and go to Bakersfield and have a ball.

One day, I went to Bakersfield. I didn't have much money to start with, and on Sunday morning I was flat broke. I called Nickie. I knew that she had money. If she would not pay train fare back to the base, I knew that I'd have to start back early because it would be impossible to catch a ride over the mountain at night. I called Nickie and explained my situation. I told her that I'd have to go back to the base that day. She asked how much the train fare cost, and I told her $1.50.

She said that I should come to see her and stay over and that she would pay the train fare. That was exactly what I was hoping she would say. We went horseback riding that day. Her horse was spirited, and I thought it would buck her off. It reared up, but she hung on and stayed in the saddle. We rode all over the place – over hill and dale!

She asked me, "Are you having fun?"

I said, "Yeah!" But I was getting pretty sore.

We went back to her place, and Nickie fed me. I had my belly full, and I felt good. I told her that I had to go catch the train. She said, "Well, kiss me again."

So, we kissed for a while, and then I said again that I had to go. Nickie said, "Kiss me again."

Finally, I figured that she had got $1.50 worth of kissing, and I went and caught the train.

One Wednesday morning, something broke down in the laundry, and we were given the day off. Holcomb and I went to Bakersfield. When we returned to base that night, we were informed that we had been transferred to CASD 4. That was Carrier Air Service Detachment 4. We were sent out to the Air Wing. We were going to go aboard an aircraft carrier, an all-Marine carrier. We were going to have to go to Santa Barbara.

For some reason, I was left out. My name wasn't on the list to go. My buddies wanted me to go with them and advised me to go see the chaplain. They said that he would help me get in.

I went to the laundry and worked for a while, and then told the ladies that I wanted to go see the chaplain about going overseas.

So, I went to see the chaplain, Captain Plant. You want to stay in good graces with the chaplain because he can help you. The chaplain went to see my captain and told him that all my buddies were going on a carrier and that I wanted to go with them. My captain then sent me to see Captain Shaefer, who was in charge of the carrier assignment. He asked me if I was stout, said it was going to be tough.

I said, "Well, I can take it!" and I volunteered to go overseas.

Because the group was not scheduled to be shipped out until the following week, I returned to the laundry and finished my week so that I could get a weekend pass.

We boarded a train for Santa Barbara. We always traveled at night so we rode a train all night.

At Santa Barbara, we were allowed to "sleep in" the first day. The next day, we went down to the line, and all the jobs were taken. There was a request for three Jeep drivers. I said that volunteering couldn't be that bad so we signed up. Sure enough, they actually wanted Jeep drivers. We were sent down to the motor pool and given some tests. Four of us were sent and there were only three vehicles, two Jeeps and a Carryall. We took turns driving. One Jeep was kept on "stand-by" for the colonel. There was not much action around there, and we switched around the vehicles. The Flight quarters were down at the bottom of the hill, and the barracks were about two miles away, on top of the hill.

At the Flight Quarters, we had to take turns on the telephone watch. Someone had to man the phones at all times. Whenever it was my turn on the telephone watch, there wasn't much to do. But, I could not tell which phone was ringing. I was a country boy and was not accustomed to talking on a phone very much. I would grab the phone and holler, "HELLO!"

The woman reservist working on the switchboard told me that she wished I would speak softer, said I was knocking her ears out.

I said, "Okay, I will."

Santa Barbara was a good liberty town if you wanted to eat. The people there wouldn't bother us much, but there was a good snack bar that was covered with all kinds of goodies – sandwiches, deviled eggs, cakes and other snacks. A lot of Sunday afternoons, we would put on a dress uniform just to go into Santa Barbara and eat.

Highway 101 came right by the main gate. We could step outside the gate and stand on the side of the road, and someone would come by and pick us up. Sometimes they would take you all the way to L.A.

I liked to go to L.A. because I wanted to go to Santa Monica. There were a lot of girls in Santa Monica, and there was a dance that lasted from dusk 'til dawn. It was a square dance. I met a lot of girls there. I also met a little sailor there. His name was Jimmy – I only knew his first name. He was from San Antonio, Texas. We buddied together, and whenever we met up on liberty, he would leave the sailors and go with me.

One time I caught a ride with a couple. Including their children and myself, there were six people in the car. The wife sat in the middle. She liked to sing hymns. She and I sang all the way to Los Angeles.

Every morning, we had to catch a bus to go pick up our Jeeps. The bus was an old Cadillac or CadiWay, which was made of plywood. An old Airdale dog always lay right in the doorway of the bus, requiring us to walk around him. He would lie in the doorway all day except when he had to use the bathroom. Then, he would jump off the bus, use the bathroom and run to the next stop, where he would jump back onto the bus.

The place was covered with dogs. We had a German Shepherd which we called "Lady." She hated civilians. Once, she had the newspaper delivery man backed up against the wall, and we had to call her off. Lady had puppies. The puppies were mixed breed but were pretty. Some of the guys carried two of the puppies down to the "slop chute" and gave them beer. Everybody was talking about how cute the puppies were, and shortly afterward, the pups were stolen.

Santa Barbara had a movie theatre. We stayed in Santa Barbara for two months. It was a good place and a good time. But, it was time to go.

Chapter Six

SHIPPING OUT

One night we loaded up on a train for San Diego. There we were to go aboard ship, the all-Marine Carrier, USS Cape Gloucester, CVE-109. We arrived in San Diego the next morning and boarded ship. We were assigned bunks and jobs.

There were 365 enlisted Marines in addition to the officers and pilots. All the enlisted Marines were new. We had no experience serving on a ship. The Marines had the air power, and the Navy was responsible for control of the ship.

We went out on a "shake down" cruise. The pilots had to qualify for carrier take-offs and landings. Each pilot had to make three landings. There were thirty-two planes on board so these qualification flights took just about all of one day.

I was assigned as a plane handler primarily on the hangar deck, which was called the V2. There were two Marines for each plane. During launch we would come up from below on the elevators to the V1, the flight deck, with our plane. People may say that was a dirty job, but actually it was an important job. The carrier could not be operated without the plane handlers. The planes have no reverse, and it was not feasible to taxi them around on a small deck. A plane would land, and the plane handlers would push it out of the way and make room for another plane to land. It was important to have plane handlers, and each plane had handlers assigned to that plane.

The planes came up from below deck. We would pull chocks until our plane came up. Then we'd help line it up for take-off. This was done in "double time."

I thought to myself, "Well, this is not so bad."

I wanted to see the plane come in and see how the hook caught the arresting cable. Therefore, I was not going to lower my head when a TBM (called a "turkey") came in. The pilot of the plane coming in was not too good, and his plane was not in position. He got a "wave off", but he was so low that the tail hook caught the cable. The plane came right over my head, and I could have reached up and touched it. The plane hung up on the side of the gun carriage with its motor running wide open. I went crawling down the catwalk on my hands and knees just as fast as I could go. I jumped up on the flight deck and came back to my station.

The plane hanging there was a new plane. One of the boys said that we should save the radar, but the captain said, "No! Get something and pry it overboard."

We had other planes in the air so we shoved it overboard and shouted, "Buy another War Bond!" (See photos.)

A Navy deck officer was responsible for signaling the planes and pilots around the flight deck. He would order the planes to move into position and this time he was leading a "Turkey" across the deck and was not aware of his situation. The next thing you knew he just backed up right off the flight deck and fell into the water, which I guess was about 40 feet below. Luckily he was not hurt and was picked up by a destroyer.

There was also a Landing Signal Officer stationed on the deck who would give the visual commands to the pilots coming in for a landing. He had two hand signal-flags and a system of signaling direction, altitude, and airspeed. When he suddenly gave the cut signal, the pilot was supposed to cut power on the engine to allow the plane to drop a bit and let the tail hook catch the arresting cable.

Behind him was an older sailor who was at least 30. We called him "Pappy" Robinson. His job was only to tell the LSO, "Wheels down – Flaps down – Hook Down!" This way the LSO would be able to concentrate totally on the flight path performance of the pilot. However, "Pappy" did not notice this one Avenger coming in who had forgotten to drop his tail hook. The plane went through all but one of the safety cables stretched across the deck, but he caught the last one, where he finally came to rest. He almost went off. He was lucky he caught that last cable.

After ten days of shake-down, we came back into dry docks. There were certain things that had to be done. One morning, I was told to grab a fire bottle and accompany a sailor who was a welder. That's all I was told so I grabbed the bottle and followed him. I lay on a bench and kidded the sailor. I told him that I had been sent down to see that he worked.

He was welding away, and then I heard someone cussing and raising sand. I never heard such talk. A guy came out and asked, "Who is the fireman?"

I stood up and said, "I am."

He told me to get my butt to the Captain's cabin. I didn't know where the Captain's cabin was located. We weren't allowed up there. But, I started up and began knocking on doors. Finally, I got to the Captain's quarters. The ship is made of metal, and the heat from the welding had given the Captain a hotfoot.

The Captain was seated behind a desk, and he went into a rage and beat on the desk. He said, "You look like an intelligent young man, but an idiot should know that if you are welding below, the fire watch should be up here! Then he continued his tirade.

Finally, I sat the bottle down and set myself at ease. I pointed my finger at the Captain and said, "Look here, Captain. I have not been to sea school. I know nothing about this ship. The only thing I've been trained to do is fight in the jungle and kill Japs. They just told me to get a bottle and follow that sailor."

The Captain cooled down then. He showed me around the ship. It was nice. After that, whenever a Navy officer would get on me, I'd just grin and relax. After all, I had seen the Captain! All the boys laughed about my giving the Captain a hotfoot, but I just did what they told me to do.

While we were at Santa Barbara, a pilot came in one day and wanted me to carry him to sick bay. I carried him up there in the Jeep and he told me to come on inside, that he didn't expect to be very long. I went in and sat down. A doctor was behind a glass front, and he looked me over pretty good. Then he came around the glass and asked me a question. He had a Yankee accent, and I could not understand him. Later, I figured that he wanted to know if I was wearing a "duty belt." But, I could never understand him. Finally, he got frustrated and shouted, "Dammit, are you wearing a gun?"

I said, "Why, no, sir."

He said, "Then take off that blankety-blank cap!"

Then we were sent to Long Beach for four or five days of fire fighting school. They would simulate fighting fire aboard a ship. They would put oil on water, and we'd have to go in and put it out. When my turn came to man the hose, I went into the cabin too far. Others were coming from other directions, and the fire was running up over my head. I thought I would be burned up before I was able to extinguish the flames.

That Saturday, I was going on liberty. When I got to the gate, I never saw so many officers with so much gold braid. I did not know what to do so I just walked on. Someone shouted, "Marine! Don't you know to salute an officer?"

I turned around and very smartly snapped a salute at him. He said, "That's better."

Another thing happened at Santa Barbara. I came into the barracks one day and left the door open. A sergeant said to me, "Shut the door! Were you raised in a barn?"

I said, "Yes, I was. And it makes me homesick to hear a jackass bray."

I thought he might get me, but he thought it was funny.

I was on liberty in Los Angeles and went into a restroom. We called restrooms “the Head.” There were several folks in there, including one soldier. I told him that McArthur had said that with the help of God and a few Marines, he would return to the Philippines. I thought the soldier was going to try to whip me.

One Saturday evening in Santa Barbara, everybody seemed to be gone. I met up with a Polish kid from Philadelphia. He said, “Rebel, let’s go on liberty together.”

I said, “How much money do you have?”

I think he and I together had $2.50. I said that we would have to go where the USO would feed us. He agreed. We didn’t know where we were going, but we took off. We stopped in Ventura, California. There, the charge for a sandwich was a dime. We didn’t want to stay there so we headed on down to San Paula. This was a Navy place, and there was a food bar with everything on it. We ate and ate.

A sailor came by and wanted us to accompany him to a small town, the name of which I can’t recall. There was to be a dance there, and he assured us that there would be plenty of girls present. I don’t know why he didn’t ask the sailors to go, but he wanted us to go with him.

The rain was pouring down. In California, they call that “liquid sunshine.” We told the sailor that we couldn’t get in the rain because our uniforms would be ruined if they got wet. He told us to stand under an awning, and he would get out and get us a ride and have the car stop to where we could run to it. He did that, and we went on to that small town.

When we got there, we were told that some bunks were available, and that we could stay there for fifty cents a night. That was right down our alley and within our price range. We stayed overnight, and the next morning the sailor and I told the kid that we were going to church. We knew that someone would ask us to Sunday dinner after church. The kid was a Catholic, and at that particular time, a Catholic could not attend services in a church of a different denomination. Catholics did not go to Protestant churches.

We told him that if we got an invitation, we would tell the folks that we had a buddy who had to be included. We went to church, and sure enough, after service, two women came up and invited us to have lunch with them. I said that we would love to do that, but we had a Catholic friend who couldn't come in church with us and he was waiting for us. The ladies insisted that we bring the friend with us, and the three of us had lunch with those two ladies. We enjoyed them, and they enjoyed us, a very enjoyable afternoon.

The sailor had a girl friend in this town, and that evening he had a date with her. She got another girl for me, and we double-dated that night. We had supper at their place. Afterward, I went back to the church, and we got to singing hymns.

The kid from Philadelphia did not go with me. He had met a married woman, and he was going to wait around until her husband went to work and then he was going to see her. I didn't like that, but that's what he did.

After we got through singing, I said that I was going back to the base. I was walking along when four girls came by and picked me up. They asked me where I was from, and I told them that I was from Alabama. Oh, they wanted to hear me talk. That was no problem because talking was my hobby. They and their families wanted me to come back the next weekend, and the girls wanted me to bring some boys. I told them that I would, but the next weekend I had some money and I went to Santa Monica where I usually went.

We stayed in dry dock for about a month, and while we were there, I went to Tijuana, Mexico. A person can get anything he wants in Tijuana. We went down there at night. Sometimes, we'd go on a Sunday. There wasn't anywhere to stay at night.

We attended a ship's party. There was beer and dancing. As we left, one of the Shore Patrolmen said something to me. I was talking with him, and my buddies got on the bus heading back to the base. I had to get on a bus by myself. As that bus got to Coronado where the ships were located, it stopped at a huge building. Even though I had no business there, I stopped and went inside the building. A sailor began kidding me about a ship. I called it a "chicken-shit ship." He got mad and jumped up. There must have been a hundred sailors there. I was lucky to get out of there alive, and I was glad to go!

The ship got out of dry dock, and we were going back aboard ship. We were loading up, and the place was as busy as a bee hive. Naturally, I was on guard duty. The Marines are always on guard duty. You know how the song goes:

If the Army and the Navy ever gaze on heaven's scenes
They will find the streets are guarded by United States Marines

The sailors would razz me while I was on guard duty. I didn't "present arms" to everybody that came up the gangplank. There was a Marine 1st Lieutenant who came up, and I failed to see him.

He grabbed me by the collar, and I quickly came to "present arms" with my rifle. If that Lieutenant had been an inch closer, he would have been saluted by his own nose. I almost hit him in the nose with my rifle. Of course, he got all over me. But that didn't bother me. I had been to see the Captain.

The Marines would call our vessel a boat. The sailors would correct us, "It's not a "boat"; it's a ship!"

It was finally time to depart. We stood on the deck and watched the horizon disappear. It gave me a funny feeling as I saw the last bit of the land. I wondered if I would ever see my homeland again.

Takeoff! The pilot receives the signal to launch. Note in the background a crewman kneels at the ready to remove wheel chocks for next plane in line to launch

Landing! The Landing Signal Officer and assistant perform their roles. The LSO concentrates on pilots flight path as the assistant verifies, "Wheels Down! Flaps Down! Hook Down!"

Actual photo sequence of a new pilot attempting landing on CVE 109 resulting in crash onto side of deck. Billy Godfrey is barely visible just under incoming plane.

Avenger Torpedo Bomber hangs precariously by one wheel and arresting cable while pilot is rescued.

USS Cape Gloucester Captain gives the order to…
"Get something and pry it overboard!"

"Buy Another War Bond!"

Chapter Seven

INTO ACTION

We went into Pearl Harbor, and we got liberty a couple of times on Waikiki beach.

We still had some pilots who needed to qualify. We picked up some new planes, Corsairs. The cowlings on the fuselage of those Corsairs were buckled. There was a bunch of officers standing around talking about what to do to correct the defect. I knew what to do. I had been in Aircraft Repair. However, I was just a PFC, and I wasn't about to go up there and tell the officers anything. All that needed to be done was to install a stringer or two. I had done that on planes where the skin was loose. At the airplane factory where I worked, if an inspector came around and found the skin loose, we had to put in stringers to tighten it up. Otherwise, the skin would buckle.

We came back to Pearl Harbor. We had some more pilot training that was required. The Corsairs were taken off the ship, and I suppose, sent back to the factory for repair. We were given some old Victory planes. These were some planes that had been used and had been put into the graveyard. But, the planes were picked up and given to us to use.

The guns on the planes were supposed to be empty. Of course, more people are killed with empty guns than any other kind. One Sunday, the ordinance man, for some reason, decided to charge the guns. We were working on the planes, all the time assuming that the guns were not loaded.

I was getting pretty dirty, and I went below to change dungarees. As I started back up and was about to stick my head up, three rounds went off in one of the guns while the plane was still in the elevator. One man who was directing the movement of the plane was hit in the head. I don't know how badly he was injured. They shipped him out so I guess he was hurt pretty badly. The bullet ricocheted and hit another man in the leg. If I had not gone below to change dungarees and had been in my usual position, the bullet would have hit me for sure.

We brought the plane down. Remember that I told about the men getting excited and stampeding during Boot Camp. Well, the guys got excited, and we could not move that plane. We were so shocked that we could not push that plane. The officer started cussing us, and that brought us back to reality. We almost pushed that plane through the wall.

Everybody was shaken by this experience. The Captain ordered that all planes be brought back to the ship, and that the ship be rigged for church. We had services, and only one of the Catholic boys was missing. The hangar deck was full of men attending church.

We went back to Pearl Harbor and picked up our planes. The pilots had to qualify for night landings by making three landings at night. We launched at midnight and when morning came, we had not recovered all our planes. In that operation, we lost three planes and three pilots. Two planes and two pilots never returned to the carrier. We figured that they were flying in formation, and one plane must have hit the other one. We never really knew what happened.

One of the two pilots that disappeared that night was a guy named Rowe. He was always drunk. There were several times he'd crawl out of his plane so drunk he could hardly walk. We joked around about him and said, "If Rowe ever dies in this war it'll be because he's sober." That night...he was sober.

The third pilot we lost that night was a Major. We called him "Smokestack" Deladio, which he didn't like that too much. He was an Italian fellow and an older pilot who had been in combat before. He got his nickname from an earlier mission where he dropped a bomb right down the smokestack of a Japanese ship.

The night we lost him, the major came in too high and flipped as he hit the barrier. He was a big, tall guy and the crash broke his neck due to that. It didn't kill him, but I imagine his flying career was over. I never saw him again.

It is well known that the Navy frequently likes to hand over the equipment they don't like to the Marines. The Navy Corsair pilots were having a really tough time making carrier landings and because so many were crashing they even considered making them land-based only. The Corsair was a great plane. It was real powerful and fast, but the cockpit was situated way back behind the under-slung gull wings. The pilots could not see anything directly below them and it was hard for them to see to drop the Corsair onto the deck. The Marine pilots got some advice from the British pilots already flying Corsairs on how to make very wide sweeping turns as they made their landing approach. Once that maneuver was learned our pilots didn't have any trouble.

We returned to Pearl Harbor and got three more planes and three pilots.

We took on supplies. Every hole or any place we could find was filled with potatoes. Later, maggots got into the potatoes. We also took on cartons, pasteboard boxes. The loading line began to get bigger and bigger. Usually the privates and PFC's do all the work, but sergeants began to get into the line of people handling the cartons. The boxes were filled with cases of beer. Everybody wanted to get in on the action. When we finished loading and took inventory, fifteen cases were missing.

Everybody was mustered in the hangar area, and search parties were sent out to find the missing fifteen cases of beer. Whenever a case was found, word was sent down to the hangar. Some of the cases were found in ungodly places. I suppose that all the missing cases were found. The beer was in plastic bottles and maybe a few bottles got out. I saw one bottle the next day.

In spite of the SNAFU concerning the missing beer, we sailed the next day to the Philippine Islands. No other vessels went with us except for a little DE (Destroyer Escort). We had to pass an island held by the Japanese. We picked up signals from submarines, and a general alarm went out. We had practiced that … practiced and practiced until we were sick of it. But, this one was the real thing! I've never been so scared in my life. I was scared, scared. But, after that one time, it never bothered me.

We had to sit up all night. We sat in the mess hall around tables, and we talked and generally "shot the bull." We told jokes.

One that I told:

A man and his wife went to the doctor. The doctor asked the man how he was doing, and the man said, "I'm doing fine. The Lord has been so good to me! Whenever I open the bathroom door, the light comes on."

The wife says, "Oh my goodness! He's peeing in the refrigerator!"

Another one:

This town was on a river. The people who lived there would confess to the priest. And they were doing some pretty awful things like going with other men's wives, etc.

The priest didn't want to hear all the details so he just told the people to say, "I fell into the river", and he would know that they had sinned.

A new priest came to town, and the people continued to confess in the same manner. The new priest got concerned about the safety hazard with all the people falling in the river. Consequently, he went to the mayor of the town and requested that a fence be built along the river.

The mayor said, "I've been here twenty years, and I never heard of anyone falling in the river."

The priest said, "Why mayor, your wife fell in three times last week!"

We survived that night and proceeded to the Philippines where we joined Admiral Halsey's Third Fleet. The large carriers in this convoy went to Japan, and the small carriers went into the East China Sea. We were operating in the East China Sea. We wore flash-proof clothing. Whenever a plane got close to our ship, we were ordered to put on our flash-proof clothing. There was a big hood that covered our heads and came down over our shoulders. We also wore gloves and goggles. A small piece of the clothing went around our mouths. The air temperature was already over 100 degrees so one can imagine how we felt in those pieces of gear.

We had more General Quarters alarms than any other ship in the fleet it seemed. The alarm went off for every little thing that ever happened. We began secretly, of course, referring to our ship's captain as "Shaky John."

Whenever a general alarm went off, I was supposed to close the hatch after the last person went down. One particular day, I went below for some reason. As I started back up, a shoe came down. I backed down, and the shoe kept coming. I hollered but the shoe kept coming. When I got to the bottom, I was pretty mad, and I started to bless the guy out. Then, I could see the lieutenant bars. Man, I went flying up that ladder, and he never found out who I was.

We operated in that area for a while. The weather was hot, and we all suffered from the heat. We got heat rash. I had never had heat rash before, but I had it on the top of my head.

It was also typhoon season in that area. June, July, and August are typhoon season in the South Pacific. The ship could not have withstood a typhoon so we had to run from the storms. We would run to avoid it, but the typhoon would still make the sea rough. The waves would be forty feet high. We had to put all the planes in the hangar and secure them with thirteen cables. A person could not walk through the hangar deck for all the cables.

If the ship was riding the waves, everything was okay. The ship would just sort of rock you to sleep. But, sometimes the ship got between waves. Then we were rolled from side to side. Sometimes the ship would be rolled so much that I would hit the chains on the side of my rack. I could feel the ship dropping, and it seemed an eternity as it went down. I would wonder if it was ever going to stop. Then I would feel the ship start to come back up. The ship would go to the left and then start over again. I had to go to the Head a lot because the rocking was hard on my kidneys.

Admiral Halsey failed to take evasive action with part of the fleet, and some of his ships were lost. Consideration was given to court martialing Halsey, but he was considered a war hero and it was thought that this would hurt the morale of the American people. We never heard about this aboard ship. And, even though he lost ships in another typhoon, Admiral Halsey was not court martialed.

We worked out there for several days. When we completed our daylight hop off, we could lie down and sleep for a little while. We had to sleep a little. We would be awakened at 3:00 a.m., and we would man our flight quarters. Sixty-four men were required on the flight deck. We had to hold our planes, and one of us had to have a fire bottle. The Corsairs would backfire and start a fire so one of us kept a fire bottle handy. Two of the men had to pull the chocks from in front of the plane's tires. As our plane moved up, the chocks would be moved up and put back in place when the plane stopped. Then the chocks would be pulled out for the plane to take off. After the plane was launched, we were free for a while. Whenever I lay down for a nap, there would be a puddle of perspiration under me when I woke up.

We had three carriers in our task force but we were the only Marine carrier. We could always beat the two Navy carriers launching, but we couldn't beat them landing. We could launch all of our planes in about 20 minutes. One morning they told us we got all the aircraft up in 18 minutes. However, we took more time to land because the Corsairs were so much bigger and had to land at a minimum speed of 90 mph and we had a lot more wave-offs as a result. The Navy carriers had the little Wildcats. They could come in at about 70 mph, a lot slower than our Corsairs.

On one occasion I just about lost my whole hand as we were launching a Corsair. Those propellers from all the planes would create a lot of turbulence. I just started slipping and began to fall, so I reached up to grab the first thing I could. Without thinking about it, the closest thing to me was the undercarriage of the wing which was coming down to get ready for takeoff on the flight deck.

Sergeant Zeiber was on the catwalk and saw what was happening but you couldn't hear anything with all the noise on deck. He jumped on the flight deck and to get me. For some reason as he was running for me he fell. He kept crawling up to me and just hit me on the leg. My immediate reaction was to throw my hand down to my side and look at him. At that very instant the wing locked into place. It still bothers me just how close I was to losing my hand. Sergeant Zeiber told me, "Godfrey, you owe me your right hand!"

When the planes were loaded with bombs and rockets under the wings we always used the hydraulic catapults to launch. The only time we didn't use our catapults was for qualifying flights. The ship would have to turn into the wind to launch and an air officer would signal the pilot to rev up his motor and then they would mash the button to release the catapult. There were three cables hooked with one to each wheel assembly and it would propel the plane to about 70 mph. Even with all that assistance the loaded plane would dip down off the end of the carrier about 20 feet toward the water, but then they would be able to pull out.

One day we had an old TBM that got his catapult shot. As the catapult released him off the end of the flight deck, his motor stalled out on him. That pilot frantically pulled the canopy off to get out and swim because here is this big ship coming right at him! We were so big we couldn't pick up a downed pilot, plus we didn't really have any way to get to him. A DE (Destroyer Escort) pulled him out of the water. Whenever a pilot was up by a destroyer he would have to stay on that ship until the carrier group went back into port.

Another day we had a Captain Fitzpatrick who came in too low. He hit a machine gun turret on the side of the carrier as he was trying to land which nearly killed the sailor in it. The left wheel of the plane was sheered off as well as his tail hook and the rear stabilizer. He had his plane looking like a grasshopper trying to get out of there. He put the throttle to it and got back up in the air. They gave him an option to try to make land if he had enough fuel or ditch in the ocean. Well, he didn't have enough fuel so he chose to ditch. We all ran out on deck to watch him bail out. He nosed the plane over and jumped out and waited for a destroyer to pick him up.

We stayed in that area for approximately forty-five days, and then went back to Okinawa. I suppose we had to re-supply. I thought, "Boy, this is nice! We won't have to get up early, and I'll be able to get a lot of sleep."

I felt like we had it made, but I was wrong! The Japanese kept us up all night. Planes would come in, and the general alarm would go off. About the time I lay back down and began to doze, the alarm would go off again. I'd jump and try to put on my britches. Everybody would be running from all directions, and I'd get knocked around. People got frustrated and started cussing. I didn't cuss. I don't take the lord's name in vain. But some would be cussing, and everybody would be trying to go out the hole at the same time. The Navy would holler, "Let the gunners up! Let the gunners up!"

The Marines would say, "To hell with the gunners!"

The attacks would go on all night, and we would be up and down, up and down. When we left Okinawa, I was glad to be back out to sea. We resumed our operation in the East China Sea. When one of the typhoons would come, we'd tie everything down and run from the storm. The storm would last about two days, and then one morning, I'd wake up and everything would be clear and smooth. I would feel so good after being in the storm. The ship would not be rocking, and the water would be just like glass.

We bombed Shanghai and shelled them. The carriers were not allowed to go close to shore. The battle wagons and cruisers went in and shelled them.

After some days, we returned to Okinawa. We were allowed to go ashore. The Navy was going to serve all of us some of that beer we had taken on in Hawaii. We caught a little landing barge and went to a small island out there. There were caves going in all directions. The Marines had taken the island, and there were still bones in the caves. Some of our boys were picking up bones, and I asked them why they were doing that. I was told that they wanted souvenirs. I said, "Why, those may be bones from American boys!"

We walked around the island, and each of us was given two bottles of beer. We were told to not mess with anything ... duds, shells or anything. But, a sailor picked up a shell and threw it into a hole. The shell exploded. I was told that the sailor's face was blown off. That sailor was not from our ship. He was from another ship in our convoy.

I was amazed at the caves that the Japanese had built on that small island. The Marines had had to burn them out of those caves.

When we returned to sea duty, we returned to the East China Sea, then to the Yellow Sea. We operated up there. On the fourth day of August, my birthday, we shot down two planes. Then we returned to Okinawa on about the ninth or tenth day of August.

We anchored in Buckner Bay. I believe it was three or four days before the war ended. On that night, the USS Pennsylvania, which was anchored right beside us, was hit by an aerial torpedo. The ship did not sink. A battleship is hard to sink. However, about twenty-three or twenty-four men were killed. The USS Pennsylvania had been hit in Pearl Harbor at the start of the war, and now it was damaged again three or four days before the war was over.

The Navy wanted all the ships out of the bay before sundown because the Japanese knew where Buckner Bay was located, and they would come in at night and bomb any ships that remained there. They wanted our ship out of the bay, but we could not hoist anchor. So, there we were – an aircraft carrier like a sitting duck. The Pennsylvania could still operate. It moved up beside us. That was good because they had more fire power than our carrier did.

All the major fleet was out. We watched them go out in the evening, and we felt pretty sad because, "You can't dig a foxhole on a steel deck!" I would have loved to be on shore and in a foxhole. But, we kept on lookout. We had received word that the Japanese were seeking peace. We didn't worry about it. We just kept watch. I did think that it would be bad to go this far through the war and get killed just a few days before the war ended.

We went up and checked the weather. We wanted it to be cloudy so that the Japs could not find us. There was the biggest full moon that I have ever seen. If we had been stateside, I would have called the moon "beautiful". But, it wasn't beautiful that night! I said, "Oh, Lord! It's a night for bombing!"

We were under more fire for that four or five days of the war than at any other time.

One night we were on battle stations, and we were told there was a "Bogey". That's what we called a Jap plane. It was approximately seventy miles out. When you hear that, you'd better start ducking. The Japanese would send one plane as a decoy, and the others would fly under the radar. About the time we heard about the Bogey, a plane came right over the mountain and hit a transport ship sitting beside us. My buddy and I were at our battle station sitting with our backs to a steel curtain. That curtain pushed us up and then back. My buddy said, "What was that?"

Jokingly, I said, "A bomb fell somewhere."

Some boys were coming down some steel stairs. They would not come down the stairs on their feet but would come down on their backsides. They told us that a Kamikaze plane had hit the transport ship next to us. I don't know why the Kamikaze plane did not hit us. Much more damage would have been caused if our carrier had been hit. We were carrying high octane gasoline, rockets, and bombs. The planes had been flown off the carrier before we entered port so we were not carrying planes.

There were not too many folks on the transport, but I think about twenty boys were killed. The transports were bringing in troops every day for the invasion of Japan. But, they had been offloaded before the Kamikaze hit.

The day that the Kamikaze hit the transport, another plane started in. All the shore batteries and the ship's guns were firing. I went to the flight deck, and it looked as if they were firing at me. I went back down and got behind a tug.

Tanks and supplies were coming into Okinawa every day. But, the atomic bomb had already been dropped. We were told that this had occurred. That was the best thing that was ever done! I know a lot of people were killed by the blast, but it saved more than it killed. If we had been forced to invade Japan, we would have had to kill women, children, old men, and old women as well as soldiers. Japanese children were being taught to stick bamboo in American soldiers. Everything was strictly military over there. The bomb saved a lot of Japanese lives.

And the Japanese would have killed every POW as soon as the invasion started. A lot of our boys were held as prisoners of war. Some had been caught in the Philippines; some were flyers who had been shot down. All these would have been killed as the first order of business as soon as the invasion began. The bomb saved more lives than it took.

I think it was the fifteenth of August when we got word. We had just finished chow, and we got word that the war was over! You talk about shouting! We were jumping up and down, whooping and hollering, shouting at the top of our lungs. A little sailor came up and kissed me right on the cheek. He said, "I want to kiss a Marine!"

Chapter Eight

RETURN TO THE U.S.A.

After the war was over, we were sent to Nagasaki. Minesweepers were sent in ahead of any American ship. We didn't trust the Japanese, and we kept planes over the minesweepers as they entered the harbor. When the minesweepers were finished, our ship pulled into Nagasaki Harbor and picked up POW's.

I could sit on the deck of our ship and look at the mountain on shore. One side of the mountain was burned, the other side was green. We did not go ashore.

There was a big Japanese carrier sitting there in the harbor. It was out of order. It had been severely damaged at the Battle of Midway.

The POW's came aboard our ship. A typhoon came in, and we had to stay in port for a couple of more days. Some of the POW's were injured. Some had a leg off, some had a hand missing. All were skin and bones. They had not been fed. I got first-hand information about how the Japanese treated our boys. I still have a hard time forgiving the Japanese for what they did to our POW's.

The boys would tell stories about how they were treated. One told of a Marine who did something which the Japs did not like. They put the Marine in a building, and just left him there. The Japanese must have given the Marine water because the other prisoners said they heard the Marine hollering for fourteen days. He could not have gone fourteen days without water. The prisoners reported that the Japanese would have the POW's line up and would just walk along and stick a bayonet in one of the guys for no reason at all.

We gave the POW's our racks. We would find a place to sleep on the flight deck or hangar. We wanted to comfort these guys as much as we could. One guy slept in my rack, and I would go by him to get into my locker. He was from Maryland. He was an orderly for the Japanese captain of the base. He did not look as bad as the rest of the guys. I suppose he got a little more food than the average prisoner got.

In that base, the water was polluted and had to be boiled before using. This orderly said that he would get the water hot, not enough to completely sterilize it. He'd catch flies and put them into the water before carrying it to the Japanese captain. The captain began looking sick, and the prisoner was asked if he was sure he had boiled the water. The prisoner assured his captors that he had boiled the water. But, he said that if the war had lasted another month, the captain would have been dead!

We gave the POW's all they wanted to eat. They wore only underwear, and their little bellies would stick out. One guy ate twelve slices of bread at one meal. We'd give them our "giddons." Those were little cups of ice cream. We'd all give our portions to the prisoners. They had not had any ice cream since the war began. We carried the POW's to Okinawa.

Then we went back to Sasebo to cover the occupation landing in Japan. That was in September of 1945. We covered the landing, and we were ordered to stand by for fifteen days. We pulled into harbor and went ashore at Sasebo. This was a pretty good-sized town, but here was nothing left! I suppose the firebombs had destroyed everything.

As we walked up the street, everybody would bow to us. Kids would salute us. One cute little boy was standing up on a bank, and he gave me the snappiest salute that I had ever seen.

We wanted a souvenir and found a back street that had not been bombed out. We began looking in the little shops and found that everything there had been made in America. We did not want little do-dads that were made in America. I finally found a gold chain. I gave thirty yen for the chain. I believe that price would have amounted to $1.50 American. I bought five dollars worth of the Japanese money, and my shirt pocket was completely filled with yen. I still have some of that money.

Today, we're begging the Japanese to build plants in the United States. I thought they ought to be begging us to build plants there. Things have turned around now. The Japanese are richer than we are.

We went back to the ship and got some carrots. When the Japanese boats would come by, we would throw the carrots at them. They would smile and bow. They probably thought we were trying to give them something. Actually, we were trying to hit them with the carrots.

After we got to Japan, we wanted to stay there because we did not know where we might be sent. We asked the ship's captain to allow the Marines to form a guard and stay in Japan. We were afraid that we'd be dropped off on some island somewhere. But, we got word to ship out. We went back to Okinawa for about ten days, and then headed for the United States.

There were about seven hundred passengers on board our ship. Cots had been put on board, and people would sleep in the hanger deck. We had left the planes in Okinawa.

I got to celebrate two Sundays in one week. When our ship crossed the International Date Line going to Japan, we lost a day. We went to bed on Tuesday and got up on Thursday. On the return trip, we got that day back. We had a Sunday before we crossed the International Date Line, and then when we crossed the line, it was Sunday again. Two Sundays in one week!

I said, "It's Sunday. I don't have to work."

I was told, "But, you had yesterday off."

There was not much to do onboard our ship so we began putting on "smokers" or shows. We practiced a "smoker" and put on a show that was enjoyed very much by all. I was the clown in the show. I had put on a sailor suit with a lot of extra hash marks on the sleeve. I wore a pair of dungarees that were about two sizes too big. I stayed on the stage all the time and, between acts, I told jokes.

One that I told:

My brother and I were hitch-hiking. We got away from home and ran out of money. We were hungry so I told my brother to wait where he was, and I would go up to the next house and try to get something to eat.

I went up to the door and knocked. When the lady came to the door, I said, "Lady, would you please give me something to eat? I'm so hungry that I could eat cold horse droppings along the way."

She said, "Why, lad. Come on in."

She fed me a good meal.

I went back and told my brother. We went to the next house, and my brother went up and knocked on the door. A man answered and my brother said, "Mister, could you please give me something to eat? I'm so hungry that I could eat cold horse droppings along the way."

The man said, "Young man, there's no need to do that. Go down to the barn and get some that are warm."

Another one that I told:

There was this couple that was uneducated. One day the husband came in and told his wife that he'd heard some folks down at the mill talking about propaganda. He asked the wife what they were talking about.

She said, "Oh, I know what they mean by that. Let me put it this way. My first husband and I had three children. My second husband and I had two children. You and I don't have any children. That means that I am the proper goose, but you are not the proper gander!"

Another one:

A little boy came home from school, and his father asked him if anything happened in school that day. The little boy said, "Well, there was one thing that happened. A little mouse ran up the teacher's dress. She caught him just above the knee, and you should have seen how much water she squeezed out of that little mouse!"

I also sang some songs, particularly the one about Old Age Pension. We had a good time, and the passengers seemed to enjoy the show pretty well. Some of them told me later that they enjoyed our show better than some of the USO shows they had seen.

After the war we had a very little to do and when the lights went out in the quarters at night. The guys would come to me and say, "Godfrey, tell us a fairy tale." The Chief Master Armorer was our boss and he would come to the hatch and even though he could not see in the dark he would say, "Alright Godfrey, I know it's you. Cut it out!"

I had that happen a lot. Many times I would get up on the hatch in the quarters area and have 50 to 60 guys around me and I'd entertain them by telling jokes and what-not. These Yankee boys have never heard these little old jokes I would tell and boy they just laughed. It just seemed like we were seventy thousand miles from home. The jokes tickled them and it helped me, too.

We stopped in Pearl Harbor and stayed about four or five days. We had liberty, and a young sailor named Taylor (from Texas) wanted to go with me. We went into a bar or tavern, or whatever they're called. I had a couple of beers and was laughing with everyone around. Whenever I got rowdy, the Hawaiian bouncer would throw me out. I don't know how many bars I was bounced from, but when I went to a bar from which I'd already been tossed, they put up a rope and refused to allow me to enter.

The ship then carried us to San Diego. Whenever you are approaching land, you'll always see seagulls before you see land. And when you see the birds, you know that land is not far away.

Chapter Nine

STATESIDE AND HOME

We went into San Diego. A band met us and welcomed us home. We got off the ship and got into quarters. We were asked what we wanted, and we told them we wanted MILK! We had not had any milk since we left Pearl Harbor. We had powdered milk, powdered potatoes, powdered everything after we left Pearl Harbor, and we had eaten all that we had.

We got the passengers off, and then re-boarded the ship and went to Coronado. There, we were given a twenty day furlough. There was no allowance for travel time. If I went home, it would take ten days to go and return to the base. I left on Tuesday. I was riding on a day coach. We were expected to lie in the aisles to sleep. I got so tired and sleepy riding all the time. I would have lain in the aisle if I hadn't been afraid that some drunk would come along and step on me.

In Texas, there was a drunk Marine. He wanted to fight everybody. There were a couple of Army MP's, Boots who had not been in the service very long. We wanted them to take care of this Marine. They would not do it. They pretended that they were supposed to only deal with Army soldiers. We called ahead and had some MP's take the Marine off at the next stop.

We got to San Antonio, and I decided to get off the train and look around. All the trains looked alike, and when I went back to the loading area, I saw a train pulling out. I thought it was my train! I ran after the train, and I was pretty fast. I ran as fast as I could, and all the while the train was picking up speed.

I caught it and saw a boy who had been with me on the ship. But he wasn't going to New Orleans. He was going to Mississippi. He said, "Godfrey, what are you doing on this train?"

I told him that I was going to New Orleans, and he told me that I was on the wrong train. By that time, the train had up so much speed that I figured I would have to go wherever the train went. Well, the train went so far, stopped, switched, and came back to San Antonio.

I got off that train and went along asking which train was headed for New Orleans. When I found it, I got on that train and did not get off again.

When we got to New Orleans, there was a one-day layover. My buddy, Holcomb, was from South Carolina, and we knew that we would have to split in New Orleans. He was going to South Carolina, and I was headed for Birmingham.

I caught the train to Birmingham and met up with some other servicemen. I had run out of cigarettes so I bummed some off a sailor.

Then, I caught the train to Gadsden. When I got to Gadsden, I hitch-hiked home. A fellow picked me up, and I fell asleep. I had not had any sleep. I left on Tuesday and got home on Saturday night. Mother and Daddy were home. I knocked on the door and hollered, "THE MARINES HAVE LANDED!"

I stayed home about ten days. When it was time for me to start back to base, we got word that my kid brother was coming home. He had been in the Fifth Army in Italy, and I had not seen him in four years. I wanted to see him. We had been very close, had dated together, and had gone everywhere together. So, I requested a ten day extension, and I got it.

I got the ten day extension on my leave, and I got to see my brother whom I had not seen in four years. I also got reacquainted with Cora Bell Grimes whom I later married. We had known each other practically all our lives. We had never really dated though we may have sat in church together when we were teenagers.

Cora Belle lived about five miles from my home. She worked in Rome, Georgia. I had not seen her in about two years so when I saw her walking down the street in Rome, we stopped and started a conversation.

I asked, "Are you married?

She said, "No, I 'm not."

I said, "How about I come over to see you?

She said, "Fine. Come ahead."

So, I went to see her.

I told you earlier about being engaged to Dorothy in Maryland. We parted company in South Carolina, and I never saw her again. The reason I never saw her again was that while I was overseas, she married a thirty-six year old sailor. I got a "Dear John letter. My buddies and I had a lot of fun with that letter. I said, "You are anybody's dog who will hunt with you!"

When the time came for me to return to base, I got on a train in Birmingham. I had a layover. The Marines had issued us a pair of kid gloves. Everybody was looking at and envying my gloves. I lay down on a bench and placed the gloves on my chest. I dozed off and when I awoke, I did not have my gloves. Some sorry, stupid clown in Birmingham had stolen my gloves.

I got on a train and headed back to California. I dreaded the long ride more going back to California than I had dreaded it coming from there. There were only straight back seats, and I could not stretch out.

A soldier got on the train. He was discharged, but he was still in uniform. He had been in Europe, but he had a brother in the hospital in San Diego. His parents wanted him to go to San Diego to see about his brother, and that was his destination.

For some reason, he had given a sailor a hundred dollars to hold for him. Four days out, I said, "Let's go back to the family car."

We went back there, and the conductor was gone or was asleep. There were two front seats that could be let out so we could stretch out our feet. We got all stretched out, and we went to sleep. While we were asleep, they cut the train in Yuma, Arizona.

The conductor came in and checked our tickets. He asked if we were going to San Diego. We told him that we were, and he said, "You're not going there now. You're on the way to Los Angeles!"

We talked about stopping and catching a later train, and the conductor told us to just stay on the train to Los Angeles. He said we could catch a taxi from Los Angeles to San Diego, and could get there before the train arrived.

The only thing that bothered me was that I was out of uniform. My hat and my bags were on the other train. But, I did have my furlough papers in my shirt pocket. When I got into the train station, I wanted to dodge the MP's. They would holler at me and ask, "Are you discharged?"

I had to tell them the story about what happened that we got cut off while we were sleeping in another car. I would try to hide and another MP would catch me. I got tired of telling that story.

The soldier and I got a taxi. We were told that the taxi would carry us to San Diego for fifty dollars. The soldier said he would pay thirty-five dollars if I would pay fifteen. I didn't have anything to lose, but I felt sorry for him so I agreed. We hired the taxi, and we were at San Diego station waiting when the train arrived.

We saw the sailor, and the soldier got his money back. The sailors told us that they had turned our stuff in to the terminal, and that we could go there to claim it. We went in, and I got my blouse and cap (piss cutter.) We got our bags. I then proceeded to the ship.

When I arrived at the ship, the Officer of the Day asked me what I was doing there. I explained about being on furlough and getting an extension. Then I was told that my outfit had been transferred to the USS Saidor, and that they had gone back to Hawaii. I was told to not worry about it because I could be flown over there. That scared me because I don't like to fly. I didn't know what to do because when I got the ten day extension, that information was never handed to my CO.

I did not have anything to show my status. I was told, "Well, Godfrey, you made corporal."

I was proud of that, but I didn't know what to do. So, I just sat down. After a while, the Officer of the Deck came by and told me that I could not stay there. When I inquired what I could do, he said, "Go to the Marine base at Miramar, California."

I found a little white, sea bag. My stuff had been carried aboard the USS Saidor. They thought I was "over the hill" or AWOL. I put what stuff I had left into that little bag and headed back to San Diego.

I met a fellow named Bayshores. I had been on a ship with him. He had also been on furlough and had gotten an extension too. We went to Miramar. The administration there had received word about Bayshore's extension, and they had his record book. They informed Bayshore that he had been promoted to corporal.

But, they did not have my book. I didn't have anything. But, they said they would bed me down, and I was given a place to sleep. I would sleep and eat. I was not asked to do any work. Since I didn't have my record book, I could not be given a job. My record book had been carried on the USS Saidor, and when they called my name, I was listed as AWOL. I lost my corporal rank. I was taken off the list, and I needed to be on it.

So, I stayed at Miramar. They never asked me to do anything. Some of the other guys asked, "Why doesn't Godfrey ever have to work?"

They said, "We can't make him do anything. We don't even know that he's in the Marines. He may just be boarding here."

I don't know how long I stayed there. I just slept and ate. All the time, I had no record book.

I met up with a Marine who had faked an ankle injury. He pretended that he broke his ankle. The ship left him but had taken his record book too. He wanted to borrow some money from the Red Cross. We went down to the Red Cross and signed our lives away. We were told that we could borrow fifteen dollars. While the paperwork for the loan was being processed, I told the Marine, "I'm going to ask them if they are sure they can spare that much."

He said, "Don't say that. They might not let us have it if you say that."

Christmas came and there I sat in Miramar. I had no money. That was the longest Christmas I ever spent in my life. There was hardly anyone on the base. I went to Christmas dinner and was served a good meal. I was given an orange and a cigar. I returned to the barracks all by myself and ate my orange and smoked my cigar.

After the first of the year, half of the boys I had been with were coming in off furlough. Half of us were let off at first, and this was the other half. I got to see them and talk with them. Then, they were loaded up and carried to El Toro. I had always wanted to go to El Toro, but I still didn't have a record book.

I sent home and asked my sister to wire me some money. She wired me fifty dollars, but I never got it. I would call, and they'd say that the money wasn't there. If I hadn't had bad luck, I would have had no luck at all.

Finally, I was called up to the office and was asked, "Godfrey, where do you think your record book is?"

I told them that it was on the USS Saidor. When they sent after the book, it didn't take long for it to arrive. It had been over a month, and when the book arrived, you can bet your life that they put me on duty right away.

I was put on guard duty. We were handling men who were going overseas. I was to guard the "Head". The outfit I was in was a "chicken shit" unit. They would not allow you to read while in the Head. I thought that was silly, but I was on guard duty. I saw a fellow sitting on a commode and reading a magazine. I told him, "You can't do that."

When I came back, he was still reading. I told him, "Fellow, I told you to put that up. It's a crazy rule, but I didn't make it. You've been a Marine long enough to know that if one of us is going to be hung, it's not going to be me! So, put up that magazine!"

Finally, he did as ordered.

Some Boots, who were destined to China, came to Miramar. I stayed in the barracks with them. Two of them were caught smoking while on guard duty. Just like Boot Camp, the whole platoon was going to be punished. An order was placed on the board for them to fall out on the grounds in dress greens. I paid no attention to the order because I wasn't a Boot. I had been overseas.

I was still in my dungarees when this "chicken" sergeant looked at me and asked why I had not fallen out in dress greens. He said, "Do you think you're better than anybody else?"

Of course, I said, "No."

He then said, "Well, get the blankety-blank in there and put on dress greens!"

So, I went in and dressed and started marching with the Boots. They were good, having just come out of Boot Camp. I had not marched in about two years. But, I was fuming. I marched along thinking about seeing everybody. Finally, a sergeant who knew me halted us. He said something to the sergeant who was drilling us, and then he called me over. He said, "Godfrey, what are you doing out here drilling with those Boots?"

I said, "That other sergeant made me drill with them."

The sergeant who knew me said that I looked tired and told me to go back to the barracks and lie down. I did exactly that.

Finally, I was told to report to Max III. This outfit was handling men coming back from overseas. The other area was about to close because the Marines weren't sending many men overseas, but instead were bringing them back.

I was told that I was a police sergeant, and I was put in charge of two "Heads". I was told that my hands did not fit anything. I was not to work. I asked about the sergeants who were coming back from overseas. I was told that they did not want to be in charge, and I was to work them. I was told that I ranked about as high as anyone on the base.

I'd go down to the line every morning and pick up my men. I'd ask for twenty-eight men. Nobody had to work very hard. Fourteen men can clean a Head pretty quickly. But, every morning I'd go down there and someone would holler, "Godfrey."

I'd look up and there would be someone with whom I'd served. It pays to be good and friendly to the guys you are over because the next time they may be over you. I'd tell them that I was in charge, and they would remind me that they had been good to me. And actually, they had been good to me. I was just kidding them.

But, there was one sergeant who I was hoping would come through. His name was Cull. He had run me up to the lieutenant for practically nothing and had called us "yardbirds." I had it planned with the 1st Sergeant that, whenever Cull came in, I was going to give him a hard time. But, Cull never did come through.

I was never much for giving orders. I had been taking orders. I was kind of easy to start with. I found out that if I didn't get tough, the troops would walk all over me. This was true, especially of those who had been overseas. They did not know that I also had been over there. One of the guys asked me, "What are you going to tell your grandkids? That you marched men to the Head?"

I jumped all over him, got on him with both feet. I learned that I had to be tough. I learned that if I could get two sergeants, one to be in charge of each Head, they could make things go smooth. They would usually be there for about two weeks. I'd get the men and turn them over to the sergeants. Then, I could go down to the guard shack and drink coffee and shoot the bull.

I got two sergeants to be in charge for two weeks. And then, I got two more. But, I had to lend one of them my blouse. He didn't have one, and I told him that I would lend him a blouse if he'd be in charge. He agreed. I told him to not let anyone cut him because he was wearing my blouse.

I stayed there as a police sergeant. You got out of service on points. Each month, they posted who was to be discharged and the number of points each of us had. Finally, they got to the number of points which I had, thirty-two points. I was going to get out in May. Boy, was I glad!

I had a girlfriend in San Diego, and she was a lot older than I was. I packed my bags and left Miramar on April 27, 1946.

They put us on a train to Los Angeles. The coaches were not air-conditioned and had straight back seats. The orange blossoms were in bloom, and we got that sweet smell. When we arrived at Los Angeles, we picked up some other boys. There were seven of us. We had not known each other previously. We had all come from different outfits. We got acquainted coming across country.

We were put on the back of the train and given a Pullman. We had a first class Pullman. We had a ball. At night there was a bed, and we'd be called when chow was ready. There was no choice with the chow. They would fix it, and we would eat what they put out. When we were traveling under orders we were allowed seventy-five cents per day and a dollar on the train. In the cafes, the waitresses did not let servicemen want for anything.

There were seven of us, and a sergeant was sent to travel with us. This was fine with me because he had our meal tickets, and we had nothing to keep up with. There was one black Marine with us. He had separate orders. I'm sure that they may have figured he would run into problems, and they gave him separate orders. We had no problem with him being black.

There was a layover in Chicago. We were in a restaurant, and some sophisticated woman about forty years old came up to me and asked if I knew the general who was seated at the next table?

I had never seen a general! So, I said, "No, Ma'm."

She said, "You mean to tell me that you boys don't know your general?"

I said, "No, Ma'm. He's never had the pleasure of meeting me."

I suppose that lady figured that we all mixed together. But, that was the first general I had ever seen. I think she wanted me to introduce her to the general so that she could flirt with him.

We caught an all-Pullman train out of Chicago going to Washington. Every car on the train was a Pullman. Servicemen were not allowed to go ahead at meals. We had to line up just like everyone else. We sat down, and I ordered something. I was told that I could not have what I ordered. Finally, I just pointed at something and said, "Give me some of that."

That night, one of the guys, Snyder, lost a shoe. He was from Chattanooga, Tennessee. I don't know what happened to that shoe. I had the lower bunk, and he had the upper bunk. He got up that morning and could not find his shoe. He was opening up curtains where women were sleeping, and they would holler. He'd say, "Has anyone seen my damn shoe?"

Snyder was down on his hands and knees in the aisle, holding up people who were trying to get to the dining car. He would look at them in a pitiful way and ask, "Have you seen my damn shoe?"

I thought that was the funniest thing, and I laughed a lot. I don't know if someone threw the shoe off the train, but he never found it. I kidded him about it. I told him that we would soon be in Union Station and that he would be out of uniform. I suggested he let me cut his foot off, and then the MP's would not bother him.

At Union Station in Washington, we had to change trains to go to North Carolina. We lost our black buddy. He had to go to a back coach. We came through Rocky Mount, North Carolina, and we had a layover there.

There was a guy in Rocky Mount who was drunk. He said that he was going to California, but he'd been there in North Carolina for a couple of days. He had money, and we didn't have any. So, we took this guy under our wings, and we went down to a place where wine was sold. The drunk guy gave me twenty dollars to buy us a bottle of wine. Just as I got there, the place closed.

We went to a small café to get something to eat. He paid for the food. The police came in and wanted to arrest the fellow, but we talked them out of doing that. We said that we would take care of the guy and not let him get into any trouble. They did not bother him while we were with him, but they may have arrested him after we left.

We then went to another town in North Carolina, arriving just after daylight. There, we shipped our sea bags home. Snyder, who had lost his shoe, had to go into his sea bag and get a pair of brogan shoes to wear home. He looked so funny in a dress uniform with brogan shoes! He was dressed like that when he was discharged. He had no other choice.

We went down to a café to eat. We had a black buddy with us, and he was not allowed in the café. We asked the folks running the restaurant to make an exception. We told them that he could sit at the table with us. But, they still refused to let him in. I did not agree with that. But, there wasn't anything I could do. Our black buddy had to go down to the bus station to get something to eat.

We were bussed over to Camp LeJeune. We never saw our black buddy again. This camp was segregated, and he was discharged at a different place than we were. We arrived at this camp on Friday, and the camp was closed over the weekend. We laid around the barracks all weekend and shot the breeze. One guy said that he had joined the service, and that he never planned to join anything again. He said that he would not even join the church if he wasn't already a member.

On Monday, they got us up and prepared us for discharge. We were shown movies and different things that we were required to see. Patches were sewn on our uniforms, and we got ready for discharge. We had to work all day, and when we go to the chow hall, it was closed. The cooks wouldn't let us in. The mess sergeant happened to see us, and he let us in. The cooks said they didn't have any more food prepared. The sergeant said, "Well, get in there and cook something! These men are going to have something to eat!" He made the cooks prepare us a good meal.

About one o'clock, we were lined up. We signed, and they paid us and gave us a discharge. We all parted, and I never saw my traveling buddies again.

I was as happy as a lark! I caught a bus to Rocky Mount. Then I caught one for Washington, D.C., and from there I caught a bus to Baltimore. I wanted to see my friends. It so happened that my former girlfriend was off work, and she had gone to spend the week with her husband in Norfolk. So, I never got to see her again.

I stayed there for two or three, maybe four days. I could have gone back to work at Martin's airplane factory. I told them that I would come back to work there, and my landlady asked if I wanted her to hold my room. I said that I wanted her to do that.

But, when I got home, I never did go back to Baltimore or to Martin. It takes a while to become adjusted after being in the service. I may have been a little wild when I got home, but I soon adjusted.

I married Cora Bell Grimes on February 15, 1947.

I went to school under the GI Bill and got my degree from Jacksonville State University in Jacksonville, Alabama.

I became a school teacher and a coach. I enjoyed being a coach more than I did being a teacher. I like kids. I hope that I had a lot of influence on some of them.

I wasn't wild anymore. I didn't do things that I did while I was in the Marines. I taught Sunday School for many years. I was choir director in my church too.

No matter what I do, I always remember Boot Camp. I may forget a lot of things, but I'll never forget Boot Camp. I belong to the Marine Corps League, and we made a trip to Boot Camp in September of 2007. We had a good time, but …

I had a little song that I wrote. It is sung to the tune of the Marine Corps Hymn:

I served in Parris Island, the place that God forgot

Where the sand is fourteen inches deep, and the sun is scorching hot.

If to heaven I should ever go, to Saint Peter I will tell,

"Another Marine reporting, sir. I have served my time in hell."

THIS IS MY MILITARY RECORD

Parris Island, South Carolina
Cherry Point, North Carolina
Oak Grove, North Carolina
Mojave Desert, California
Santa Barbara, California
San Diego, California
USS Cape Gloucester, CVE-109
Pearl Harbor
Philippine Islands
East China Sea
Okinawa
Nagasaki, Japan
Sasebo, Japan
Camp Miramar, California
Discharged at Camp LeJeune, North Carolina

I have an Asia-Pacific ribbon with two battle stars for the East China Sea and Okinawa Campaigns. I also have a Presidential Unit Citation with one star.

Editor's Note

The publisher requested verification of the actual name for Billy Godfrey. He stated that his name is Billy Sandel Godfrey which he gave himself since his birth certificate reads only B S Godfrey. His parents had in mind that he be named after the famous evangelist of the era, Billy Sunday. However, they just used the initials on his birth certificate. "I was always called Billy growing up so I just kept that and added the family name Sandel. I was never William or anything other than Billy."